READY FOR TAKEOFF
TAKEOFF

Opportunities in Aviation

GRACE KIMANI
Aviation Facilitation Expert

This book is fondly dedicated to my son, Gareth. Your presence in my life has been a source of constant joy and inspiration.

Thank you for choosing to embark on this incredible journey of life with me.

For those who are seeking opportunities to position themselves advantageously, may this book serve as a beacon, guiding you towards your desired direction. It is my hope that the knowledge and experiences shared within these pages inspire you, challenge you, and ultimately lead you to your unique path in the aviation industry.

CONTENTS

ACKNOWLEDGMENTS

I WISH TO EXPRESS my heartfelt gratitude to all those who made the creation of this book not just possible but a truly enriching and rewarding journey.

Firstly, I bow my head in thanks to the Divine for blessing me with the precious gift of life, for it is through this gift that all other achievements are possible.

Tony, the esteemed CEO of Proavia Consults, deserves my sincere appreciation for his insightful contributions drawn from his expertise in the aviation industry. His wisdom and guidance were invaluable during the writing of this book.

My profound thanks go to Geofrey Semaganda. His challenge to me, to transform my two decades of experience into a book with the potential to educate and inspire, was a call to action I am deeply grateful for.

I am also immensely thankful to the diligent team at Wealth Messenger. Their dedication and attention to detail resulted in this beautifully compacted book that now reaches your hands. The seamless blend of their talents made this manuscript a polished gem.

I owe a significant debt of gratitude to my mentors in the Aviation sector. Dr. Rose Koros, Joseph Okumu, Abel Gogo, and Gad Kamau. Their mentorship and inspiration in various aspects of aviation have played an instrumental role in shaping my career and this book.

BACKGROUND

READY FOR TAKEOFF: Unlocking the African Aviation Industry's Potential, by seasoned aviation expert Grace Kimani, serves as a guided tour into the untapped vistas of the African aviation sector. Boasting nearly two decades of industry experience, Grace deftly explores the vast opportunities lying beneath the surface of this sector, debunking the age-old perception of aviation being limited to roles like pilots, air hostesses, and aeronautical engineers. Drawing from her personal journey, she illuminates the diverse spectrum of opportunities aviation offers.

The book emerges as a lighthouse of inspiration and guidance for students contemplating their future career choices. It uncovers the wide range of professions nestled within the industry beyond the aircraft - from accountancy and hospitality to engineering and human resources. Grace challenges the view of aviation as a bastion for the privileged, portraying it instead as a sector open to all who exhibit determination and ambition.

For entrepreneurs, *Ready for Takeoff* offers a refreshing look at the crossroads of aviation and other industries, for instance, agriculture. It disentangles the intricate aspects of import and export within aviation, demystifying misconceptions that have made such activities seem exclusive to a select few.

Grace notes that although aviation information is often cocooned within aviators' circles, she aims to dismantle these barriers, making this knowledge comprehensible to anyone interested. Whether it's interpreting data from international entities like IATA and ICAO, identifying educational and business opportunities, Grace's insight is easily accessible to all.

Moreover, the book underlines the transformative power of technology on the industry, especially post-COVID-19. It highlights the vital role technology will play in revolutionizing the industry and creating more prospects for budding professionals and entrepreneurs.

Ready for Takeoff: Unlocking the African Aviation Industry's Potential isn't merely a captivating walkthrough of the aviation industry. It's a clarion call to students, parents, guardians, entrepreneurs, and aviators to view the industry as a vast ocean of opportunities ready for exploration. Grace employs her firsthand experience and comprehensive knowledge to equip her readers with the tools they need to venture into and thrive in the world of aviation.

CHAPTER ONE

A BEGINNER'S GUIDE TO AVIATION: CRAFTING A CAREER IN THE SKY

FOR COUNTLESS AVIATION enthusiasts, the dream of turning their love for flying into a livelihood is both thrilling and attainable. The prospect for future commercial pilots is indeed promising. Rapid expansion of the global commercial jet fleet, unprecedented demand for air travel, and a limited labor pool prompted Boeing to predict a need for 790,000 pilots over the coming 20 years in 2018 [Source].

Many of us harbored dreams of becoming pilots in our youth. Navigating a massive aircraft across the sky and journeying around the globe sounds like the most thrilling job one could have. Launching a career in aviation is a possibility at any age, but there are several essential steps to ensure your successful entry into the industry.

To thrive in the aviation sector, you'll need to cultivate specific personality traits and obtain necessary compliance credentials. Upon completing your training, you can then decide if a long-term commitment to this industry suits you. The silver lining is that the field of aviation is a veritable universe of opportunities!

Therefore, amassing as much experience as possible and meticulously logging it is crucial. For instance, pilots need a substantial amount of flying experience before they can secure their dream job! Nevertheless, no matter which path you embark upon, it's essential to know how to market yourself as an industry expert.

Before we buckle up for this exhilarating journey, let's first lay the groundwork.

Understanding the Aviation Industry

Typically, "aviation" refers to air travel, specifically in a plane. While airplanes and helicopters are the most prevalent types of aircraft, modern definitions of "aviation" now include the operation of unmanned aircraft, such as drones. The usage of drones saw a substantial rise from 2019 onwards, especially for delivering essentials like food and medicine during the Covid-19 Pandemic when travel restrictions were in place.

Before the pandemic struck, Zipline, one of the world's premier drone delivery services, had been refining its drone delivery system for lightweight crucial supplies in Rwanda and Ghana. They had been collaborating with authorities more open to embracing drone technology in their airspace than those in the United States, the European Union, and other larger Western democracies.

These endeavors established a system that could be swiftly scaled up when the pandemic started. By June 2021, Zipline CEO Keller Rinaudo announced that the company had delivered at least 2.6 million COVID-19 vaccine doses in Ghana, planning to deploy over 2.4 million more by the year's end, particularly in remote and sparsely populated areas.

In Rwanda, where Zipline's system is most mature, the company primarily delivers blood, medical supplies, and personal protective equipment (PPE). In February 2021, it began round-the-clock operations, enabling hospitals to place orders at any hour.

In East Africa we have Dronector Academy located in Kenya that is introducing and launching students to unmanned aviation career as an opportunity in Africa.

Therefore, the aviation industry encompasses everything related to air and space operations.

The ABCs of the Aviation Industry

Among the most globally entrenched industries, aviation forges connections between people, cultures, and businesses across continents. Colleagues within this industry work relentlessly to augment the understanding of aviation's role and its numerous benefits. To maximize the advantages of air travel and bolster aviation's sustainable growth integrating more people and regions it's imperative for all stakeholders and partners to cooperate.

The aviation industry of today envelops a wide array of airtravel components as well as the activities supporting them. This includes the entire airline sector, aircraft manufacturing, research organizations, military aviation, and much more. This book aims to enlighten you about everything pertinent to aviation and the encompassing industry.

Whether they are pilots, engineers, air traffic controllers, maintenance staff, or safety officers, the aviation industry depends heavily on a highly skilled workforce. The growing demand from emerging economies may lead to a potential scarcity of skilled labor in the mid-term. Longer-term, we might witness more fundamental alterations in the nature of work, with shifts towards on-demand labor, leveraging new systems to mold employees to work as per their convenience.

Industry's Key Players

An 'airline' is a company offering air transport services for passengers or cargo, and the 'airline industry' is the overarching term for all such companies. The airline business, however, forms only a fraction of the overall aviation industry. Besides airlines, the aviation industry includes aircraft manufacturers, research firms, air safety experts, military aviation companies, and increasingly, businesses engaged in drone design, production, or utilization.

Economic Impact of the Aviation Industry

As per the Aviation Benefits Without Borders' publication from December,2024, the Air Transport Action Group(ATAG) reports that the aviation industry supports approximately 87.7 million jobs globally, either directly or indirectly through the industry's supply chain, expenditure of its workforce, and the aviation-enabled tourism industry.

11.3 Million Direct Employment Opporutnities

Directly, the aviation industry employs roughly 11.3 million people in roles such as:

- 648,000 airport technicians (working for the airport operator)

- Other airport-related jobs: 5.5 million (retail, car rental, customs and immigration, freight forwarding, and catering)

- 3.6 million airline employees (flight and cabin crews, executives, ground services, check-in, training, maintenance staff)

- 1.3 million in civil aerospace (engineers and designers of civil aircraft, engines, and components)

- 237,000 air navigation service providers (air traffic controllers, executives)

These roles are 4.3 times more productive than an average job in the broader economy.

18.1 Million Indirect Jobs

Indirectly, aviation supports over 18.1 million jobs worldwide through its consumption of goods and services. These include roles in air transport industry suppliers such as fuel suppliers, real estate developers, aircraft system integrators, airport goods manufacturers, and various customer service roles like call centers, IT, and accounting [source].

13.5 Million Induced Jobs

Employees in the air transport industry (direct and indirect) globally support 13.5 million induced jobs through their personal consumption of goods and services. Their purchasing power contributes to job creation in retail, consumer goods, and a variety of service sectors such as banking institutions and restaurants.

Tourism Sector: A Workforce of 44.8 Million

Tourism is rapidly evolving into the most significant industry, with air transport playing an indispensable role in its growth. Current assessments indicate that aviation buttresses around 44.8 million jobs within the tourist sector.

Importance of the Aviation Industry

The aviation industry has notably contributed to global economic prosperity. This isn't merely due to the stimulation of regional economies through tourism, but also due to the enhancement of global commerce. The steadily burgeoning employment within the aviation sector directly engages millions of people worldwide in diverse roles, from pilots and cabin crew to airport security and aerospace engineers. Moreover, the aviation industry has contributed to the creation of numerous jobs within the broader travel and tourism sector.

Role in E-Commerce

Air transport empowers global trade and e-commerce by facilitating the globalization of manufacturing. While air freight comprises a small volume of world trade, it represents significant monetary value. In 2024 , air transport was projected to reach 115 million metric tonnes nearly 9% year on year increase worth of goods globally, making up 35% of worldwide trade by value.

Influence on the Manufacturing Industry

At present, air transport carries nearly 90% of business-to-consumer (B2C) e-commerce shipments. From2019 to 2024, e-commerce's share of scheduled international mail tonne kilometres (MTKs) surged from 9% to 19.9% with a forecast to reach 26% by 2030.

Contribution to the Medical Industry

Thanks to dependable air transport services, people have access to essentials needs with improved living conditions, food, medicine, education, safety, and more. Aviation remains the safest and most efficient long-distance mode of transportation globally. Many remote communities depend on it as their only means of transportation to access health care and food supplies. Air transport serves as a reliable mode of transporting emergency humanitarian aid to those impacted by natural disasters, famine, or war. In rural or peripheral areas, air transport acts as a lifeline service, offering connectivity that would otherwise be lacking.

Impact on the Education and Health Industries

Additionally, aviation simplifies access to education for students worldwide, particularly those from developing countries seeking better education abroad. By broadening visitors' leisure and unique experiences, aviation contributes to enhancing their quality of life. It enables people to visit distant relatives and friends at affordable costs and promotes cultural understanding.

In terms of long-term development, air transport could significantly influence regions like Africa, which houses nearly 15% of the world's protected areas, endowing Africa with a significant comparative advantage in attracting international tourists. The development of nature-based tourism (eco-tourism) could serve as a profitable enterprise and employment opportunity while assisting in the preservation of natural reserves.

Categories of Aerodromes and Airports

Various airport frameworks have been established globally to enhance productivity, efficiency, and profitability. However, the presence of a certain facility type in one country does not guarantee its existence in another due to factors like political instability, religious and economic sanctions, and security concerns.

Commercial Service Airports

In civil aviation, both commercial and private aircraft are used for cargo and passenger transport. These airports are typically bustling year-round, hosting flights from around Africa. Notable examples include Jomo Kenyatta International Airport, O.R Tambo International Airport, Addis Ababa Bole International Airport and Murtala Muhammed International Airport.

Cargo Service Airports

According to the Civil Aviation Authority(CAA), for an airport to be classified as a 'Cargo Service Airport,' it should have at least 100 million pounds of cargo capacity.

These airports specialize in handling all aspects related to cargo, such as shipping and various other deliveries.

Civil and Military Aviation Airports

Military aviation generally supports aerial combat or surveillance missions and other military operations. Most military aviation is affiliated with air forces, but other divisions exist, such as army aviation, navy aviation, and coast guard aviation.

Widely used Aircraft Around the Globe

There exists an extensive list of various aircraft types worldwide, each designed to serve distinct purposes. To understand the diverse nature of these aircraft, it's essential first to comprehend how they are categorized. Broadly speaking, aircraft fall into two categories: Aerostats, which are lighter than air, and Aerodynes, which are heavier than air.

Aerostats (Lighter than Air)

These aircraft operate similarly to ships, utilizing buoyant force to navigate the air. They are filled with a low-density gas such as hydrogen, helium, or hot air to achieve lift. As the name suggests, this low-density gas is lighter than the surrounding air. Common examples of aerostats include blimps and sky parasols.

Aerodynes (Heavier than Air)

In contrast to aerostats, aerodynes are substantially heavier and larger in mass and volume. They achieve lift by propelling gas or air downwards, which in turn propels the aircraft upwards. Aerodynes are characterized by their dynamism, derived from the momentum of air. This dynamic lift is primarily generated by engines.

Helicopters

Helicopters, colloquially known as choppers, fall into the rotorcraft category. Their lift and thrust are generated by horizontally rotating rotors. These aircraft offer the unique advantage of being able to take off and land vertically, move forward, backward, and laterally. They can operate in varied locations and fly over populated areas, unlike certain fixed-wing aircraft. The size, purpose, and function of the helicopter determine its engine type. Today, helicopters serve numerous purposes, including military, cargo, construction, rescue, surveillance, and public sector tasks.

Gliders

Gliders, a type of fixed-wing aircraft, primarily derive their lift from the reaction of air against their lifting surfaces. Gliders typically employ a wheeled undercarriage for takeoff and landing. Once primarily used for military purposes, gliders now serve recreational and tourism-related activities. Popular glider types include hang gliders and paragliders.

Civil Airplanes

Civil aircraft encompass all non-military airplanes, including private and business planes, as well as commercial airliners.

Private Jets

Private jets, often single-engine monoplanes, are used for recreational flying. These aircraft can vary widely in their sophistication, including nostalgic "warbirds" (ex-military aircraft flown for sentimental reasons) and aerobatic planes, which are designed for high maneuverability and sport events.

Business Aircraft

Business aircrafts range from small, single-engine planes used for pilot training or short-range transport to four-engine executive jets capable of traversing continents. They are employed by professionals from diverse fields, including salespeople, explorers, farmers, doctors, and clergy. Primarily, they are used to optimize the time of top executives by liberating them from commercial airline schedules and traffic. In addition to serving as a valuable tool for prospective clients, they also provide a premium perk for executives.

Other commercial aircrafts have diverse uses, including agricultural activities, traffic reporting, wildfire fighting, special operations, pipeline monitoring, cargo transportation, and a host of other tasks.

Fighter Jets

Fighter jets, commonly known as fighters, serve as a crucial component of military aviation. These are specialized fixed-wing aircraft, designed predominantly for air-to-air combat against other aircraft. Notable for their impressive speed and maneuverability, fighter jets were initially conceived to counter air-based threats. Nonetheless, some fighter aircraft have extended capabilities, allowing them to conduct ground attacks, earning them the title of "jet fighters." The evolution of technology has resulted in modern fighter jets equipped with sophisticated enhancements, including advanced communication systems, cutting-edge sensors, secure cockpits, and bandwidth efficiency among other features.

Cargo Planes

Also known as freight planes, airlifters, or cargo jets, they are distinct fixed-wing aircraft purposed primarily for transporting cargo or freight. These planes are meticulously designed with specific features that support lifting and transporting heavy loads. Unlike passenger aircraft, cargo planes are devoid of amenities for passengers, focusing solely on efficient cargo transport. Notable features include large doors for easy loading and unloading, facilities to ensure shipment protection during transit, and high wings that help keep the cargo close to the ground. Furthermore, cargo planes typically have more wheels to support their heavy load. Both civil and military operations widely use these versatile aircraft.

Career Opportunities in Aviation: More Than Just Piloting

Working in the aviation industry doesn't limit one to only becoming a pilot; it offers a wealth of opportunities across a large, diverse team. The industry encompasses various roles, each requiring a unique set of skills.

Technical positions such as pilots, navigators, technicians, or engineers cater to those with a knack for machines and technology. But the career opportunities in aviation don't stop here. Let's explore the extensive range of jobs available in this sector, the responsibilities each entails, and the potential remuneration:

The Spectrum of Opportunities

The aviation industry forms an integral part of the global transportation network, providing a rapid solution for international trade. It not only bolsters economic growth and job creation, but also promotes global trade and tourism. The thrill and convenience of flying, facilitated by the aviation industry, has helped build global relationships, bridging geographical gaps and fostering significant economic advantages. Alongside these benefits, the industry has made remarkable strides in improving flight safety and addressing evolving security challenges.

With the advancement of communication technology, e-commerce, and potential application of 3-D printing, some air travel could be replaced or its growth influenced. However, transporting passengers and goods over vast distances remains indispensable for long-term development.

Sustainability remains at the core of the industry's approach, striving to meet people's economic and personal needs while preserving the capacity for future generations to fulfill their own. This delicate balance hinges on a thriving economy, a strong global community, and a clean environment capable of supporting over seven billion people. Factors such as regulatory frameworks, technological advancements, and energy costs will also shape future growth.

Modern aviation and aircraft manufacturing firms are focused on designing more efficient aircraft to safely cater to increasing demand. Today's aircraft are around 80% more energy-efficient per passenger kilometer compared to those produced in the 1960s, and this trend of increasing efficiency is set to continue with each new generation of aircraft.

The aviation industry's focus on technological innovation has considerable societal benefits. The returns on R&D "research and development" investment in the aerospace industry are projected to surpass those of the overall manufacturing sector. Every USD 100 million invested in research yields an additional USD 70 million in GDP benefits annually.

Tourism and Aviation

Air travel plays a pivotal role in the thriving global tourism industry. It's estimated that over half (58%) of all international tourists travel by air, demonstrating the symbiotic relationship between aviation and tourism industries for long-term growth.

The tourism industry benefits greatly from aviation, both in terms of employment and contribution to GDP.

Direct Impact

The expenditure of international tourists arriving by air is estimated to support approximately 19.6 million jobs globally. These jobs span several sectors such as hospitality, restaurants, visitor attractions, local transportation, and car rental, excluding jobs in the airline industry itself.

Indirect Impact in the African Context

Tourists arriving by air facilitate an additional 16.4 million jobs within industries that cater to the tourism sector. These direct and indirect tourism roles spurred by air transport further generate seven million jobs in other sectors of the African economy, as employees spend their income on goods and services. Tourism significantly contributes to Africa's economy, supporting job creation and economic development.

E-Commerce has revolutionized logistics, and Africa has not been left behind. As online companies and consumers demand faster deliveries, shipping models have adapted to these needs.

Aviation plays a vital role in this transformation. According to Willie Walsh, IATA's Director General, air cargo handlers managed 39% of eCommerce traffic increase in 2024 . This has shown African corporations the ease and efficiency of air freight transportation, prompting a rise in the industry as it capitalizes on e-commerce.

Air cargo now accounts for 35% of global airline revenue due to increased demand. E-commerce contributes 20% to 25% of global air cargo volume and expected to rise to 30% by 2030. This transition, marked by the emergence of 'preighters,' signals the industry's evolution towards a more cost-effective, convenient, and automated future.

Perks of Working in the Aviation Industry

Travel the World

Working in aviation presents a unique opportunity to explore the world. While it might be demanding, few industries offer more travel options. Roles like pilots and flight attendants often involve significant travel, visiting numerous locations across continents in a short period. Even when not working, aviation workers often benefit from reduced-price or even free flights, making travel more affordable.

Making New Friends

Working in the aviation sector, you become part of something larger, keeping pace with a vibrant and fast-evolving industry. This dynamic environment offers daily variety and constant interaction with new people, adding to the appeal of working for an airline or airport.

The Chance to Advance Your Career

Airlines and airports have a vested interest in the continuous improvement of their staff, often providing opportunities for training and professional growth. Some airlines, for example, maintain a team of development specialists who assist staff with their career progression, hosting courses, and providing resources to aid advancement.

Renumeration Benefits

Airport jobs provide excellent remuneration and outstanding benefits. Some incentives are unique to their airports, like discounted holiday parking fees, while others focus on employee commuting needs.

Lifestyle Perks

Recognizing the importance of work-life balance, airlines and airports provide benefits that extend to employees' home lives. They offer child benefits, family leave, high-street store discounts, subsidized nursery places, and more. Health and retirement benefits are also prioritized, with reduced fee health cash plans and robust pension plans being part of the attractive perks for long-term employees.

Conclusion

The aviation industry, including airports, is governed by stringent safety and security regulations, making it one of the most heavily regulated sectors worldwide. Safety focuses on maintaining internal industry standards, typically operational, while security is about preventing external threats, usually human-related.

With the numerous benefits of working in the aviation sector, it's no surprise if you've decided this is the right career path for you. Whether you're looking to break into the aviation industry or already employed and looking to advance, there are a myriad of opportunities awaiting in Africa's vibrant aviation sector.

LESSON 1:

Exploring Careers In Aviation

Introduction: Your Sky Is Bigger Than You Think

When most people think about aviation, their minds immediately picture a pilot in uniform, confidently walking through an airport terminal. For decades, this image defined success in the industry. But aviation is far more expansive than the cockpit. Behind every safe take-off and landing is an army of professionals engineers, safety inspectors, meteorologists, air traffic controllers, business analysts, and even digital marketers.

In fact, the International Air Transport Association (IATA) notes that the industry supports more than **87 million jobs globally**, with less than 5% of these being pilots. This means 95% of aviation opportunities lie elsewhere. For Africa, a continent with one of the youngest populations in the world, this is both a challenge and an open door.

This lesson is about helping you broaden your view. Instead of asking, *"Can I become a pilot?"* you should be asking, *"Where in aviation can my skills make the greatest impact?"*

Deep Dive: Careers Beyond the Cockpit

1. **Aviation Operations:** From ground handling to airport operations, these professionals keep the system running smoothly.
2. **Aviation Safety & Security:** With global threats evolving, airports need highly skilled safety managers, auditors, and crisis responders.
3. **Engineering & Technology:** Drone operators, aerospace engineers, and software developers are rewriting aviation's future.
4. **Customer Experience & Marketing:** Airlines are competing on passenger comfort, digital convenience, and loyalty programs.
5. **Entrepreneurship in Aviation:** From air cargo startups to drone delivery

services, Africa is witnessing a rise in aviation-based businesses.

Case Study: In Rwanda, **Zipline** employs hundreds of staff not as pilots, but as logistics planners, drone operators, maintenance specialists, and customer service agents. Their mission: deliver blood and medicine to remote hospitals. It's a perfect example of how aviation careers can save lives.

Exercises

1. **Career Mapping:** Write down five aviation roles that interest you. Use online resources (IATA, ICAO, LinkedIn) to check the entry requirements.
2. **Strengths Match:** List your top three skills (technical or soft) and connect them to aviation roles. Example: "Good at problem-solving → Aviation Safety Analyst."
3. **Future Self Activity:** Write a one-page scenario of where you see yourself in aviation ten years from now. Be specific

about the role, country, and kind of impact you'd like to make.

Action Framework: Your Career Flight Plan

1. **Research Training Options** – Identify one training program, academy, or university relevant to your chosen role.
2. **Network Early** – Join at least one aviation association (Women in Aviation, Young Aviators Club of Africa, or a LinkedIn group).
3. **Build a Skills Portfolio** – Start with free or low-cost online courses (e.g., aviation safety, drone technology, customer service excellence).
4. **Seek Mentorship** – Approach a professional in the industry to guide you.
5. **Start Small, Dream Big** – Volunteer at an airport, aviation expo, or drone club to gain exposure.

Reflection Journal

- Which three aviation careers excite me the most?
- What existing skills can I apply in aviation today?
- What's one step I will take in the next 90 days to move closer to my aviation dream?

CHAPTER TWO

THE GLOBAL AVIATION SCENE WITH AN AFRICAN PERSPECTIVE

IN ANY INDUSTRY, change is the only constant, presenting unique challenges on the horizon. Unforeseen innovations or policy changes can disrupt the most established sectors, with the transformations being abrupt or gradual. Navigating these changes can prove tricky, often lethal for organizations failing to actively plan for them.

A study conducted by an independent aviation research entity, Aviation Benefits, unveiled that air transport and its supporting sectors account for approximately 12 million jobs and 63-75 billion in direct and indirect revenue within the African landscape. This demonstrates a growth from the previous decade, encapsulating 2.2% of total employment and 2.7% of Africa's combined GDP.

As of 2024, the African Aviation sector employed over 750,000 individuals, with a breakdown suggesting that:

- 57% were directly employed by airlines in roles such as pilots, cabin crew, customer service officers, and more.

- 10% served in airport management, security, customs, and similar roles.

- 30% worked in airport retail stores, hotel services, taxi services, restaurants, among others.

- 5% held technical roles including aircraft manufacturing, engine checks, inspections, etc.

- 2% worked on advanced systems like air traffic control and engineering.

A Glimpse into the Future

The future of aviation appears promising, given the industry's exponential growth. As the only rapid global transportation infrastructure, aviation promotes economic development, job creation, and stimulates international trade and tourism.

Aviation, now recognized as a global strategic asset, plays a critical role in achieving the UN (SDG) Sustainable Development Goals. Forecasts suggest the industry's growth, with the most conservative estimates predicting an average annual increase in air travel demand of 4.3 percent over the next two decades.

Our industry has evolved immensely over a century, from early efforts to fly faster, further, and heavier aircraft, to currently managing 100,000 or more commercial flights globally every day – signifying over 400 departures per hour! This technological progress has made aviation one of the world's most reliable and safest transportation modes. Advancing and improving productivity standards in aviation and all transportation forms will enhance the emerging mobility sector's performance and sustainability, instilling public confidence and promoting long-term viability.

Moreover, technological innovation is vital in redefining the efficiency of travel. Cutting-edge technologies, such as autonomous vehicles and ultralight materials, present possibilities to transform the mobility system by enabling new business models and services. Developments in unmanned aerial vehicles, (AI) artificial intelligence, biometric identification, mechatronics, blockchain technology, renewable energies, and electric aircraft are just a few examples. Consequently, aviation stands at the forefront of the innovation conversation, steering the potential implications on new mobility options.

However, the surging demand for air travel presents fresh challenges, particularly significant logistical implications across airports to accommodate this growth. The paramount concern is how we can progress in a responsible and sustainable way.

Given the industry's plan to nearly double passenger and cargo numbers by 2036, there is an expected surge in demand for drone operators, engineers, airline pilots, and other aviation-related professions. It's certain that technological innovations and strategic approaches will be necessary to sustain this growth which calls for promoting the next generation of aviation proffessionals.

Performance of Aviation: A Worldwide Outlook

As civil aviation embarks on a new phase of trials, it becomes crucial to evaluate the industry's and service's global maturation, along with the elements that could significantly influence its future trajectory.

Air transport connects the world, from ferrying passengers from Athens to Zambezi and sustaining livelihoods along these routes. This segment explores the impact of the aviation sector on global economies, job creation, and operational activities within various regions and institutions around the world.

In Africa, Aviation Industry supports 12 million jobs, with aviation-enabled tourism constituting roughly 80% of all employment. The economic growth of several African nations heavily reliant on the steady inflow of foreign visitors hinges on the connectivity afforded by aviation.

The Asia-Pacific region boasts the highest passenger traffic levels, accounting for more than one-third of global passengers.

Europe, contributing one-quarter of worldwide passenger traffic, is the second-largest market globally, following only the Asia-Pacific region.

In Latin America and the Caribbean, aviation accounts for 2.7 percent of the workforce and produces 3.5 percent of total economic output.

Emerging on the scene, the Middle East anticipates a 4.1 percent increase in traffic control over the next two decades, marking the highest growth rate worldwide. In North America, air transport fosters 2.7 million jobs within the aviation sector and supports 8.8

million jobs. Small island nations often heavily depend on the revenue from tourism enabled by the aviation industry. The business and growth interactions facilitated by aviation-enabled tourism form a crucial component of regional industries within developing nations.

For every individual directly employed within the aviation industry and aviation-enabled tourism, an additional 5.9 million jobs are indirectly supported in other Organisation for Economic Co-operation and Development (OECD) nations.

In the European Union (EU28), 5,087 aircraft are operational, managed by 234 airlines, and carry 903 million passengers. Air transport in the EU28 propels 9.8 million jobs and $794 (€672) billion in economic growth.

The Asia-Pacific Economic Cooperation (APEC) air transport sector employs 6.7 million individuals.

This growth trend is projected to continue for the foreseeable future due to various factors, including potential economic growth, urbanization, education, job opportunities, among others. With the expansion of air transportation, market opportunities escalate. As urbanization increases, residents can secure well-paying jobs enabling them to travel abroad for professional development and leisure. Presently, it is estimated that 10% of the population can afford the cost of international travel.

Performance of Aviation in the African Market

Of all the major markets, the African aviation sector presents the most opportunities for growth. This is because it is a nascent industry with a large and burgeoning population.

However, this potential may not fully translate into an increase in air traffic. According to ICAO's long-term traffic forecasts, passenger traffic in Africa is projected to grow around 4.3 percent per annum until 2045, marginally faster than global growth. Similarly, freight traffic in the region is predicted to outpace the global average, at 3.9% per year over the same period.

a)Safety & Security

Ensuring safety in African air travel remains a challenge that the region is striving to overcome. A majority of aviation incidents can be attributed to lack of training, lax enforcement of protocols, and scarcity of necessary skills. However, concerted efforts are being made by the International Air Transport Association and the International Civil Aviation Organization to enhance African aviation.

b)Declining Infrastructure

Africa's air transport industry faces considerable challenges due to outdated and inadequate infrastructure, shortage of skilled personnel, and transport facilities. While significant improvements have been observed, the industry is striving to compete with larger international airports worldwide.

c)Lack of Communication & Recognition

Despite the aviation sector being a major contributor to Africa's GDP, it is not considered a priority by several African governments. Many are still hesitant to seize the opportunity to establish national airlines. Due to a lack of recognition for local aviation skills, experts prefer to migrate abroad and attain international acknowledgment.

For instance, Kinshasa, the capital of the Democratic Republic of the Congo, is one of Africa's largest cities, with a population larger than London and a skyline spanning across the Congo River. However, nonstop flights from Kinshasa to Lagos, Nigeria's commercial hub and Africa's largest city, are non-existent. The two megacities are approximately 1,100 miles apart, akin to the distance between New York and Minneapolis. Yet, no direct flights are available. A traveler must change flights at least once, spending upwards of $1,200, with the journey likely exceeding 12 hours.

This narrative is common across Africa. Commercial flights are sparse, pricey, and circuitous. An African passenger often has to undertake an extensive detour, transiting through the Middle East or Europe to travel from one African nation to another.

Role of Aviation in UN-SDGS (Sustainable Development Goals) In Africa

Air travel is integral to Africa's prosperity as it unlocks opportunities previously non-existent or unexplored. With a global hub via aviation, numerous African regions and countries would be interconnected, leading to a substantial rise in trade, cultural exchange, and business.

a)SDG in Employment & Diversity

With recent changes in airline and aviation regulations, employment in this sector has emerged as a positive economic activity worth $56bn, providing approximately 12 million jobs in Africa. However, challenges such as high jet fuel consumption, taxes, and departure fees have somewhat hampered the growth of Africa's aviation industry.

b)SDG in Gender Equalityin the Aviation Industry

Aviation and Gender Equality Aviation is making strides to alter gender balance across the sector. However, more work is needed to improve the gender ratio in fields such as engineering and ramp operations. General Electric (GE) Aviation's initiative, Cultivate, aims to develop and retain female engineers in the company. The program has already achieved gender equality in its engineering development project at a 50:50 ratio.Women remain underrepresented in senior leadership roles in businesses, governments, and the corporate sector across Africa and the world. The International Air Transport Association (IATA) aims to reverse this trend by 2025 through its "25% by 2025" campaign. The initiative aims to achieve gender balance in international aviation, starting with IATA's head office and expanding to airlines.

The campaign endorsed by 59 airlines, including Air Botswana, TAAG-trans air Angola, Turkish Airlines, Air France, and British Airways. These airlines committed to increasing the number of women in management positions and jobs where they are underrepresented, such as avionics and operational roles, by 25% annually. To track progress, annual reports on diversity and inclusion data will be generated.

c)Sustainable Goals and Aviation Sustainability In Food

Every day, consumable agricultural products are airlifted. Aviation also aids in delivering crucial humanitarian aid to areas affected by natural disasters and war through organizations like the World Food Program. The UN World Food Program, through the UN Humanitarian Air Service, transports critical food stocks to war or disaster-stricken areas in a timely and safe manner.

Aviation and The Global Supply Of Clean Water Conventional cleaning methods for turboprop planes can consume up to 13,000 liters of water. Still, new 'dry wash' methodologies can reduce this by up to 95%. As with any industry, aviation must be mindful of water use, particularly in water-stressed areas.

d) SDG in Aviation and its Efforts in Combating Climate Change

The aviation industry has committed to an ambitious CO_2 reduction strategy and is making significant progress towards three global climate goals. Due to collaborative efforts through new products and improved operations, the same flight today produces about half the CO_2 it would have in 1990. The long-term goal of aviation is to cut its net CO_2 emissions by half by 2050, relative to 2005.

Emergency and Disaster Response In air transportation plays a critical role in providing aid, medical supplies, food, skilled personnel, and more. With the right infrastructure and trained staff, rescue, cargo, and refugee transfer operations can be successfully conducted.

e) SDG in Preparing the Next Generation of Aviation Professionals in Africa

i)Attracting Young Minds

Several approaches have been employed to attract, empower, and educate the upcoming generation in the aviation industry. The ICAO's Next Generation of Aviation Professionals (NGAP) initiative works to ensure the right training of the workforce, the development of infrastructure, job opportunities, transportation, education, and more.

ii)Artificial Intelligence (AI) in Aviation

At its core, AI is a branch of computer science aimed at automating tasks and even simulating human intelligence in machines. AI has proven to be a valuable tool in the aviation industry, performing repetitive, time-consuming tasks, and extracting valuable information from large data sets. Airport operators are particularly interested in AI due to its potential for improving air traffic control and capacity optimization.

AI is the future, and we are gearing up for it. It's anticipated that AI technology, through various forms of machine learning, will surpass human intelligence and bring about significant change. AI can make training and scenario handling more robust, whether for combat or civilian aircraft.

Major companies are witnessing significant shifts as AI continues to evolve. AI-powered virtual assistants are helping airlines enhance the efficiency and competitiveness of their pilots by automating routine tasks. AI systems can also predict maintenance needs even before a part fails, leading to prompt repairs and minimized downtime.

How is the Aerospace Industry Revolutionizing the Aviation Industry?

Aerospace, a technologically advanced industry concerned with both aviation and space travel, has proven to be a diverse area of study with numerous military, industrial, and commercial applications. The global aerospace market is booming with many new startups entering and transforming the industry.

Take SpaceX for instance. Founded in 2002, this American space transportation services company has the goal of reducing space transportation costs to make Mars colonization possible. The company's worth at $74 billion as of 2021 is still growing.

Commercial space travel, like any novel domain, requires innovation. Elon Musk leading this innovation, striving to fund the concept of space exploration. His ambitious plans of launching a prototype of a new spacecraft and completing the first full flight of the spacecraft and its booster. He aims to establish a fully functional city on Mars by 2050.

In conclusion, whether it's through integrating AI into everyday tasks, improving education and training, or innovating in commercial space travel, the next generation of aviation professionals in Africa has an exciting future ahead. They'll have the opportunity to make significant contributions to technological advancements and the transformation of the aviation and aerospace industries.

Drivers of Change for the Aviation Industry

a)Climate Change

Climate change and extreme weather conditions are among the most pressing challenges facing the aviation industry. The frequency and severity of weather events such as wildfires, temperature extremes or storms are predicted to increase. These events can disrupt infrastructure and displace communities, leading to flight cancellations and delays, higher operating costs, and compromised safety.

b)Cybersecurity

Cybersecurity is a significant concern as more of the industry's operations and systems are digitalized. From ticketing to air traffic control to onboard systems, the aviation industry presents a variety of targets for cyber threats. In addition, the increased use of data for personalized passenger experiences and operational efficiency raises concerns about data privacy and protection.

c)Alternative Energy Sources & Fuels

The search for sustainable and alternative energy sources is driving change in the aviation industry. Efforts to develop biofuels and electric aircraft are underway to reduce the industry's environmental impact and dependence on fossil fuels.

d)Consumer Preferences

Consumers are demanding more personalized and convenient experiences, along with sustainable practices. This has led to the development of more customer-centric services, sustainable practices like carbon offsetting programs, and innovation in areas like ticketing and in-flight services.

d)Supply-Chain Integration

The integration of the air-industry supply chain is another driver of change. Technology is enabling greater transparency and efficiency in the movement of goods, parts, and people. However, it also introduces new challenges in managing complex networks of suppliers, logistics providers, and manufacturers.

e)Geopolitical (In)Stability

Geopolitical instability can lead to travel restrictions, safety concerns, and fluctuations in passenger demand. This instability, combined with issues like terrorism and transnational crime, has led to increased security measures and protocols, impacting everything from passenger screening to cargo handling.

f)High Oil Prices

Although there's been efforts towards lower oil prices, any future rises could significantly impact an industry where fuel costs typically represent a substantial portion of operating expenses. It could lead to increased fares and reduce demand for air travel.

g)Strength and Volatility of the Global Economy

The strength and volatility of the global economy influence demand for air travel, both for tourism and business. Economic shifts, like the rise of emerging markets and growing inequality, can change trade patterns and consumer behavior.

h)Environmental Activism

Public concern about the environment is causing industries, including aviation, to rethink their practices. Airlines and airports are investing in cleaner technologies, adopting more efficient practices, and engaging in initiatives to offset their environmental impact.

In conclusion, the aviation industry is facing a host of drivers of change, from climate change and cybersecurity threats to shifting consumer preferences and geopolitical instability. Addressing these drivers successfully requires agility, innovation, and a commitment to sustainability and customer-centricity.

A Balancing Act In Aviation Industry

In the coming decades, advances in connectivity and sensor networks are poised to empower citizens with real-time access to information and unprecedented transparency. Conversely, privacy concerns and the risk of espionage will inevitably climb the agenda for governments and military organizations.

Data Privacy and Surveillance: The question that arises is: how much privacy will people be willing to relinquish in return for convenience, economic benefit, and enhanced security? The rise in cyber-attacks and cybercrime will necessitate novel data security measures for businesses, potentially turning privacy into a treasured and sought-after commodity. This brings out more innovative job opportunities due to evolving trends like;

a)The Evolving Face of Terrorism

Terrorist organizations have demonstrated an alarming capacity to adapt to the strategies and procedures employed by counter-terrorism agencies and intelligence services. The democratization of technology might well give rise to a shift away from state-sponsored political terrorism towards disparate, flexible operations. Terrorist groups often find fertile ground in nations characterized by weak governance, ethnic, cultural, or religious divides, weak economies, and permeable borders. But what will the challenges of

tomorrow look

like, and will they be manifest in the virtual or physical world?

b)Evolving Global Regulations on Emissions and Noise Pollution

Despite varying levels of optimism in predictions leading up to 2050, the aviation industry's contribution to global CO_2 emissions remains relatively low compared to other forms of transportation. The question arises: will standards like the ICAO CO_2 emissions standard, coupled with advancements in technology, operations, and infrastructure, be sufficient to meet global climate goals?

c) Evolving Threat of Pandemics and Infectious Diseases

We once believed many infectious diseases were under control, but the emergence of new threats like HIV, SARS, and Zika virus, alongside animal diseases such as BSE, have reminded us of our vulnerability. Even prior to recent pandemics, Africa's aviation sector faced significant challenges, from a lack of air transport deregulation to inadequate airports and limited air traffic management capabilities. The aviation sector has nonetheless proven essential to the continent's economic development due to terrestrial transportation infrastructure shortcomings.

Conclusion

As customer expectations become more demanding, service industries will be compelled to evolve. Success is to those capable of preempting, addressing, and providing solutions to customer issues before the customer is even aware of them.

The aviation industry's journey has been truly remarkable - a journey spanning just over a century. We've evolved from learning to fly to operating faster, more extensive, and more advanced aircraft. Today, we're handling over 100,000 commercial flights daily, which translates to an astounding rate of over 400 departures per hour!

The aviation industry has been a forerunner in technology adoption, leveraging advances to enhance efficiency, safety, and customer experience. As a result, it has evolved into one of the world's most reliable, efficient, and sophisticated modes of transportation.

But, the industry's evolution doesn't stop here. As we face the future, we look forward to leveraging new technologies and innovations to continue improving, reducing our carbon footprint, increasing connectivity, and opening up more opportunities worldwide. Whether it's making travel more affordable or expanding our reach to the farthest corners of the earth, the goal is to serve the global community better and drive economic and social growth.

The future of aviation will likely be shaped by ongoing advancements in artificial intelligence, automation, and sustainable fuel options. These innovations will not only improve efficiency but also address the critical issue of environmental sustainability. As the sector continues to grow, its commitment to reducing emissions and noise pollution will remain a top priority, impacting future technological innovations and regulatory standards.

The aviation industry will also need to continue adapting to global trends and challenges, such as the demand for increased data privacy, evolving security threats, and the risk of pandemics and infectious diseases.

In the face of these challenges, the industry's resilience and ability to innovate will be key to maintaining its role as a vital part of the global transportation infrastructure.

LESSON 2:

Aviation In A Global & African Context

Introduction: Africa's Aviation Future in a Global Sky

Every day, more than 100,000 flights link cities across the globe. Yet Africa, with 1.4 billion people, still represents under 3% of global air traffic. This imbalance is both a limitation and an opportunity. Aviation is more than transport it's a driver of trade, jobs, tourism, and innovation. Understanding global trends while grounding them in African realities is key to shaping the continent's aviation future.

Deep Dive: Global Growth vs. African Challenges

1. **Global Expansion:** Passenger demand will rise 4.3% annually for the next 20 years, led by Asia-Pacific and the Middle East.
2. **Africa's Opportunity:** Infrastructure gaps, high fees, and limited intra-African

routes slow growth, but potential is unmatched.

3. **Tourism Dependency:** 80% of Africa's aviation jobs link directly or indirectly to tourism.

4. **Sustainability Mandate:** Aviation is tied to climate goals, requiring greener fuels, smarter airports, and sustainable growth.

5. **Innovation Push:** AI, drones, biometrics, and blockchain are transforming operations Africa can leapfrog by early adoption.

Case Study: The Single African Air Transport Market (SAATM) was launched to liberalize Africa's skies. If fully implemented, it could add $1.3B in annual GDP, create 155,000 jobs, and lower ticket prices. Yet fewer than half of African nations have ratified it, showing the challenge of regional cooperation.

Exercises

1. **Global Benchmark:** Compare two countries (e.g., Ethiopia vs. Singapore)

in aviation performance. Identify three differences in policy, routes, and innovation.

2. **Connectivity Design:** If you were starting an airline, list three intra-African routes you'd prioritize and why.

3. **SDG Mapping:** Pick one Sustainable Development Goal (e.g., Gender Equality, Climate Action). Explain in one page how aviation in Africa could accelerate it.

Action Framework: Plugging Africa Into the World

1. **Stay Informed:** Track SAATM, AfCFTA, and ICAO guidelines they set the rules of the skies.

2. **Think Regional:** Focus on underserved African routes to boost intra-continental travel.

3. **Adopt Green Practices:** Explore electric planes, biofuels, and carbon-reduction strategies early.

4. **Forge Partnerships:** Link African operators with global players (IATA, Boeing, Airbus).
5. **Youth Inclusion:** Advocate for young professionals in forums Africa's demographic dividend is its edge.

Reflection Journal

- Which global aviation trend excites me most (AI, drones, green fuels, connectivity)?
- How can Africa transform its aviation weaknesses into opportunities?
- If I had the chance to advise my government, what one aviation policy would I push first?

CHAPTER THREE

AVIATION MANAGEMENT BEYOND PILOTING

WHEN ENVISIONING A CAREER in the aviation industry, most GenZ often see themselves as pilots. However, the industry offers a plethora of roles that are as vital as piloting. An aviation management degree, Diploma or its equivalent equips students with the preliminary technical and managerial skills required for entry to aviation space.

Upon completing this courses, students are prepared to take up diverse roles where they learn on job training the comprehensive operations in various areas in Aviation industry. . This includes supervising flight and ground operations, cargo and baggage handling, and coordinating flight and ground crew members among others

Inside Aviation Operations

The Aviation Management program prepares students to efficiently handle airline and airport departments. With the ever-soaring heights that aviation management continues to reach, the industry has immense potential. For instance, India has the world's third-largest civil aviation market, according to aviation data analytics economic times 2024.

Aviation management encompasses several domains including ground handling, fleet management, booking, hospitality, tourism industry boards, and in-flight services. The prospect of a career in airline operations is appealing due to its vast growth potential and opportunities extending beyond Africa. Working in an industry that allows traveling worldwide for a living could indeed be a fulfilling job.

Aviation management involves coordinating and managing the logistics and operations of an airport, airline, or other aviation-related roles. The field has diverse aspects and oppotunities, some focusing purely on logistical issues like fleet planning and airport traffic handling, while others focus on airline marketing and flying-related services. Both commercial airlines and aerospace manufacturers heavily rely on aviation management.

Blossoming Careers in Aviation

Aviation is a flexible industry brimming with opportunities for fresh talent. Working in aviation may not always come with fixed working hours, but it promises endless possibilities.

Many aspire to work in the fast-paced aviation industry and for a good reason. A career in aviation offers not just the thrill of exploration but also several perks from job stability to flexibility.

Teamwork is crucial in aviation. The industry demands likable personalities with technical expertise. After all, each flight carries the responsibility of ensuring passengers' safety and comfort. Therefore, essential skills for aviation professionals include teamwork, reliability, mental presence, language proficiency, motivation, clear speech, physical fitness, and health.

Those aspiring to work as ground crew or flight attendants in international airlines can qualify with a bachelor's degree in any field. However, roles such as technicians or pilots require a science degree. Various certificate courses like Diploma in Aircraft Maintenance and Diploma in Aviation Hospitality are also available for those keen on joining the aviation industry.

a)Aviation Security

Aviation has always been considered a potential target for terrorist activities. However, the 'one-size-fits-all' approach to aviation security adopted by many countries has been ineffective against the ever-evolving threats.

Threats to aviation come in many forms, and it is imperative to identify, assess, and devise suitable mitigations for them at a localized level in addition to following guidelines set by authorities.

A critical element of this is ensuring that airports are safe. A Security Management System (SeMS) provides a set of corporate philosophy and guidelines that help improve security performance by proactively managing risks and identifying potential weaknesses.

Career Prospects in Aviation Security

Aviation security management roles demand a combination of team leadership, a comprehensive understanding of airport security protocols and systems, and hands-on experience. Candidates for these roles typically possess a bachelor's degree in fields such as business or criminology, and having previous work experience in protective or security services can be advantageous. Additional experience within the aviation industry can also give a job candidate a significant edge.

Airport security professionals are entrusted with critical responsibilities that include safeguarding terminals, aerodromes, aircraft, and other aviation infrastructures against illegal threats or actions. They ensure the safety of all buildings, technology, material, and equipment owned by the airlines, government, and non-government organizations within the airport and aerodrome premises. They are responsible for ensuring adherence to Aircraft Rules, including supervision of surface vehicles and drivers within the airport and aerodrome boundaries.

Furthermore, they play a pivotal role in maintaining overall law and order within the airport and aerodrome premises in coordination with the police, taking cognizance of all offenses committed within the boundaries under any existing law.

b)Aviation Quality Control and Assurance

In aviation, quality assurance (QA) plays a critical role in building customer trust. It ensures the products and services meet high-quality standards before they are provided to customers. The QA department in the aviation industry makes sure that all activities, including civil aviation, maintenance tasks like checks, repairs, safety inspections, and personnel training are performed according to specific regulations and standard practices.

In business and industry, the concept of quality assurance has been applied for many years, signifying excellence and compliance with standards. It reflects an unwavering commitment to certain standards that lead to consistent product quality that meets specific customer requirements.

c) Aviation Business Oppotunities

Manufacturers in the aviation industry often face challenges including undefined customer requirements, lack of clear communication regarding expectations and constraints on required services, a culture with subpar safety standards, limited resources, and undefined process relationships. An effective quality management system takes these challenges into account and provides solutions that help enhance service quality and meet the required standards.

d)Aviation Safety

Aviation safety jobs employ various strategies to ensure the safety of aircraft, operational procedures, air traffic, flight traffic, and all other aviation-related aspects. It can even encompass passenger behavior and the rules of conduct during flight.

Aviation safety professionals utilize advanced research, training, best practices, regulations, and comprehensive investigation. In the aftermath of an unfortunate incident, aviation safety experts can contribute by deciphering the sequence of errors and mishaps. Comprehending what went wrong on a problematic or crashed flight aids in preventing similar future incidents.

Safety Management System requires the practitioners to embrace safety culture, safety reporting, safety awareness, safety communication and readiness to ensure safe working environment and safe skies.

Safety Management Job Requirements

The most effective route to becoming an aviation safety practitioner is through relevant skills and work experience.

Career Opportunities in Aviation Safety

i)Aerospace Engineers

Aerospace engineers make decisions about what can fly in the sky and space. They are responsible for ensuring the ongoing safety of manufacturers' aerospace and space products, including airplanes and spaceports. Their work typically falls into two areas: aircraft certification and commercial space transportation.

ii)Aviation Safety Technicians/Officers

Aviation Safety Technicians provide technical assistance to safety inspectors during audits or investigations.

iii)Aviation Safety Analyst

Safety analysts help interpret data related to aviation safety. They not only assess current aircraft for potential risks, but also contribute to designing and conducting these assessments. This role is ideal for someone who enjoys research, has strong mathematical skills, and can discern larger patterns in data.

iv)Aviation Safety Inspector

For those who dislike being desk-bound, the role of inspector offers more movement. While aviation safety inspectors do complete paperwork, their duties can vary depending on their specific role. Ultimately, inspectors help evaluate safety compliance with Civil Aviation Regulations.

v) Aviation Safety Business Opportunities

Changing trends in Aviation Industry brings newer specifications for various air operators to ensure safe operations as per ICAO requirements on Safety Management Systems and Aircraft Maintenance Management .

These two areas create mega business opportunities for manufacturers and also create numerous jobs.

Air Traffic Controllers: Air Traffic Controllers are the unsung heroes of the aviation industry. They are responsible for managing the movement of aircraft within an airport's airspace, ensuring optimum safety and efficiency. Their tasks involve coordinating aircraft Takeoffs and landings, directing aircraft on the ground, and monitoring the aircraft within their control zones. They act as the 'eyes and ears' of the pilots, assisting them in navigating through congested airspace, avoiding other aircraft, and dealing with adverse weather conditions. The role of an air traffic controller is immensely challenging and requires high concentration, decision-making ability, and excellent communication skills.

Aviation Meteorologists: Aviation meteorologists play a crucial role by providing vital weather information and forecasts that are essential for flight planning and safety. Weather conditions significantly affect all aspects of aviation operations, from flight safety to scheduling and fuel efficiency. These meteorologists use advanced technology and tools to predict weather conditions such as turbulence, wind shear, icing conditions, and storms, helping pilots prepare and adjust their flight plans accordingly.

Cabin Crew: Often the most visible face of the aviation industry to passengers, the cabin crew, which includes flight attendants, is responsible for the safety and comfort of passengers during a flight. Their duties extend beyond serving meals and refreshments. They brief passengers on safety procedures, manage any in-flight emergencies, and even provide first aid. In essence, they ensure that passengers have a safe and pleasant flight experience.

Ramp Agents: Ramp agents, also known as aircraft ground handlers, carry out a wide range of duties on the airport tarmac or ramp. They handle the loading and unloading of baggage, guide planes to and from their gates, and perform inspections and minor repairs. Their responsibilities also include marshalling aircraft, de-icing planes, and servicing aircraft lavatories. These individuals play an essential role in maintaining the smooth flow of airport operations.

Aviation Psychologists: Aviation psychologists are experts in understanding the behavior of pilots, air traffic controllers, and other aviation personnel. Their research can lead to improvements in training programs, safety procedures, and the overall well-being of those involved in aviation. They study factors such as stress, fatigue, and human error, and their implications on performance and safety in the aviation environment.

Aviation Consultants: Aviation consultants are experts who provide advice and solutions to airlines, airports, and associated businesses. They can specialize in diverse areas such as operations, safety, environmental impact, financial performance, regulatory compliance, and strategic planning. These consultants use their in-depth knowledge and understanding of the aviation industry to help clients improve operational efficiency, mitigate risks, and enhance profitability.

Airport Managers & Operation Managers: They have a broad and comprehensive role in overseeing all operations at an airport. This includes managing safety and security, ensuring compliance with regulations, coordinating with airlines, supervising staff, overseeing customer service, and managing the airport budget. In addition, they play a pivotal role in emergency planning and response.

Aircraft Leasing Managers: Aircraft leasing managers oversee leasing transactions for aircraft, engines, and other equipment. Their tasks involve contract negotiations, managing relationships with lessees and lessors, and ensuring compliance with leasing terms and conditions. They play a key role in managing the financial and operational aspects of aircraft leasing, contributing to the economic viability of airlines.

To sum up, these roles, among many others, contribute to the smooth and efficient operation of the aviation industry. Each of these professions requires a unique set of skills and specialized knowledge, illustrating the diversity, complexity and the limitless opportunities within the Aviation space.

Airport Facilitation Roles

Airport Authorities: An airport authority is an autonomous entity responsible for the management and supervision of one or several airports. The authority is typically guided by Directors and C.E.O who is/are appointed by high Government Authority i.e. the President.

State Agencies: They are the Oversight Authority, commonly known as (CAA) Civil Aviation Authority as guided by ICAO. State agencies work closely with airport authorities to regulate the aviation industry. They enforce aviation laws and regulations and are responsible for issuing permits and licenses to operate within the industry. They also conduct safety inspections and investigations, ensuring compliance with safety regulations and standards.

Catering Agencies: Working in airline catering requires a specific set of skills and abilities. The tasks are diverse, ranging from food preparation, packaging, and transport to ensuring adherence to safety and Airline policies guided by IATA regulations. Roles include food prep employees who cut and chop food, assemble meals, and package them for shipment. Delivery drivers transport meals and beverages from the airport kitchen to the aircraft, ensuring timely arrival. The ability to work in a fast-paced environment, excellent communication skills, and physical endurance are essential in this field.

Administrative Roles

Airport Stakeholders and Concessionaires:

Airports involve a diverse set of stakeholders, each with different interests and objectives. Cooperation with stakeholders leads to improved passenger and cargo facilitation which enhances customer experience. addressing their concerns and integrating their feedback. Building trust among stakeholders can make them more open to the necessary adjustments and concessions in airport projects.

Airport Concessions: These typically involve a contractual relationship between the government, as the asset owner, and the private sector concessionaire. They offer various services that are much needed by travelers and airport users. There are numerous job opportunities offered by the sector.

Perks of Working in the Aviation Industry

Career Advancement: Starting a job in aviation management often involves extensive training, helping you develop invaluable skills for the rest of your career. Moreover, the industry frequently offers opportunities to learn new technologies, gain industry certifications, and participate in seminars and conferences.

Global Opportunities: Aviation management provides an opportunity for international exposure. Not only does the job potentially offer travel opportunities, but the skills learned are transferable across borders, making overseas work opportunities more common.

Cultural Diversity: As an aviation worker, you'll interact with a wide range of individuals from various cultures. This allows for exciting experiences and knowledge expansion, promoting both personal and professional growth.

Travel and Vacation Benefits: Many aviation positions offer substantial travel and vacation benefits. These can range from flight discounts to savings on car rentals, rail tickets, and hotel stays.

Conclusion

Aviation career opens the door to employment opportunities with path to national and international work experience.. It allows proffessionals to interact with day-to-day operations of airlines and airports, providing them with a varied and exciting work environment. Career advancement within the industry can be influenced by your area of specialization combined with your attitude and experience.

In addition to high compensation, working in the aviation industry provides numerous benefits such as health insurance, vacation time, annual leave, and free or subsidized air travel. Some companies offer generous retirement plans, free travel passes, and cost-effective vacation planning services.

LESSON 3:

Aviation Management Beyond Piloting

Introduction: The System Behind Every Flight

While pilots capture the spotlight, the hidden engine of aviation is management. Behind each safe departure is a network of managers coordinating safety, operations, customer experience, and logistics. Aviation management ensures that planes depart on time, baggage is delivered, customers feel cared for, and regulations are met. This lesson shows how management careers shape aviation and how you can position yourself to thrive in them.

Deep Dive: Core Domains of Aviation Management

1. **Operations Management:** Overseeing flight schedules, turnaround times, baggage flow, and day-of-operations control.

2. **Safety & Security Leadership:** Running Safety and Security Management Systems (SMS/SeMS) to prevent risks.

3. **Quality Assurance & Compliance:** Auditing processes to meet ICAO and IATA standards.

4. **Customer Experience (CX):** Managing passenger journeys, service recovery, and satisfaction.

5. **Business & Strategy:** Driving profitability through commercial planning, concessions, and cargo optimization.

Case Study: *Ethiopian Airlines* didn't become Africa's largest carrier by pilots alone. Its growth came from disciplined management: investment in training, world-class safety systems, and well-run logistics operations.

Exercises

1. **Role Research:** Choose two aviation management roles (e.g., safety officer, operations manager). Write down

qualifications and skills needed for each.

2. **Scenario Drill:** Imagine a storm delays all departures. Draft a 1-page plan covering communication with passengers, crew coordination, and safety checks.

3. **Skill Match:** List your three strongest skills (e.g., organization, problem-solving, communication). Map how each could fit into aviation management.

Action Framework: Building Your Aviation Management Path

1. **Learn:** Explore diplomas, degrees, or certifications in aviation management, safety, or operations.

2. **Certify:** Take ICAO or IATA certifications in SMS, quality assurance, or airport management.

3. **Intern:** Apply for internships or volunteer roles at airports/airlines to gain exposure.

4. **Network:** Join aviation associations (ACI, Young Aviators Africa, AWICA).

5. **Specialize:** Pick one management domain (safety, operations, Customer Experience, quality) and create a 5-year career plan.

Reflection Journal

- Which management role excites me most, and why?
- What personal strengths could I apply in aviation management today?
- If I had to lead an airport team during a disruption, how confident would I feel?

GRACE KIMANI

CHAPTER FOUR

EXERCISING LEADERSHIP IN THE AVIATION INDUSTRY

LEADERSHIP IS THE VITAL ingredient of success across organizations, and its importance is particularly accentuated in the domain of business aviation. Here, we provide valuable tools and insights aimed at helping executives in business aviation refine their leadership skills and lead their organizations towards their goals. Remember, leadership is not restricted to positions of authority or those in managerial roles; leaders can emerge from any rank or file.

Africa's aviation industry is a significant contributor to its economy, creating about 12

96

million jobs and generating $80 billion in economic output. The industry comprises about 731 airports and 419 airlines. The International Air Transport Association (IATA) forecasts that Africa will emerge as one of the fastest-growing aviation markets in the next two decades, exhibiting an annual growth rate of more than 5%.

Mr. Juan Carlos, the 12th Secretary-General of the International Civil Aviation Organization (ICAO) from August 2015 to 2021, reiterated the tremendous potential of the African aviation industry. This potential can be realized through the execution of regional commitments and the pivotal role aviation plays in countries' response to and recovery from global pandemics.

The International Civil Aviation Organization (ICAO) is a specialized agency of the United Nations, funded by its member states. It establishes principles and techniques of international air navigation and fosters planning and development of international air transport to ensure its safe and orderly growth.

The agency has its headquarters in Montreal, Quebec, within the Quartier International.

The ICAO Council develops standards and recommended practices concerning air navigation, its infrastructure, flight inspection, prevention of unlawful interference, and facilitation of border-crossing procedures for international civil aviation. Additionally, the ICAO prescribes the standards and regulations necessary for the safety investigation of aviation accidents and incidents.

Once standards and recommended practices are adopted by the ICAO's Commission, they are presented to the Council, the political arm of ICAO, for consultation and coordination with member states, followed by final approval. ICAO distinguishes itself from other international air transport organizations as the only one having regulatory power among its member states. Other international organizations include the International Air Transport Association (IATA), representing airlines, and the Civil Air Navigation Services Organization (CANSO), representing air navigation service providers.

IATA The International Air Transport Association (IATA) was formed in 1945 as a trade association serving airlines. Its role in establishing industry standards and hosting tariff conferences that served as a platform for price-fixing earned it the label of a cartel. As of 2016, IATA's member airlines, comprising 290 airlines, most of them being major carriers serving 117 nations, carried about 82% of total available seat miles air traffic.

IATA supports airline activity and helps formulate industry policies and standards. It is headquartered in Montreal, Canada, with executive offices located in Geneva, Switzerland. IATA, representing 290 airlines in 120 countries, now stands as a global trade organization for the aviation industry. Despite the evolving aviation landscape, marked by privatization, alliances, and intense competition, airlines continue to work collaboratively to provide a seamless and high-quality product to customers.

Almost every nation has a Civil Aviation Authority (CAA), but their existence usually comes to the fore only when an incident occurs. They work behind the scenes in the aviation industry, monitoring operations, and setting and enforcing safety standards. There are numerous civil aviation authorities worldwide, the most notable being the Federal Aviation Administration (FAA) in the United States, established in 1958 to regulate and oversee the burgeoning airline industry.

Other well-known civil aviation authorities include Transport Canada's Civil Aviation Directorate (TCCA), the Civil Aviation Authority (CAA) of the United Kingdom, the Civil Aviation Administration of China (CAAC), and the European Aviation Safety Administration (EASA).

What Are The Responsibilities Of Civil Aviation Authorities? While the responsibilities vary from country to country, common functions of CAAs include being government or quasi-government bodies, dealing with civil aviation traffic, formulating safety standards that can be legislated by their government superiors, and enforcing these safety standards.

In essence, most CAAs establish, oversee, and enforce safety standards in their local aviation industry, applying to airlines based in their countries and those flying into their airspace. The CAA plays a pivotal role in maintaining and enhancing aviation safety standards, continuously striving to make long-term improvements in aviation systems, culture, capabilities, and operations.

Moreover, the CAA stimulates competition to benefit passengers, leading to more affordable flights, greater choices, and enhanced insurance coverage. The CAA also plays a role in mitigating the environmental impact of the aviation industry. This way, it meets specific criteria to remain effective and efficient while also adding value to the industry it serves.

Aviation Regulatory Authorities and their Role in Ensuring Safety

An aviation regulator, typically referred to as a National Aviation Authority (NAA) or a Civil Aviation Authority, is a government agency responsible for overseeing and regulating civil aviation within a country. Several hundreds of such regulators exist worldwide, each working towards implementing and upholding the standards set forth by the International Civil Aviation Organization (ICAO), a specialized agency of the United Nations committed to fostering worldwide connectivity.

Roles and Responsibilities of CAA

Being national bodies, the responsibilities of aviation regulators can vary based on the specific needs and demands of individual countries. However, primary responsibilities typically include maintaining an aircraft register and issuing certificates of airworthiness for aircraft. This register provides crucial information about an aircraft and plays an integral role in ensuring the safety and security of air travel.

Additionally, aviation regulators often work towards ensuring that key standards are met to guarantee air travel safety. This involves setting standards for aircraft and maintenance services, licensing personnel, and influencing the industry. While some aviation authorities are responsible for investigating airplane accidents, others may handle air traffic control. In certain countries, the national aviation authority also plays a role in developing and managing airports.

International Aviation Regulators

The global regulatory landscape is complex, with several entities governing the operations of air travel. The International Civil Aviation Organization (ICAO) stands as a specialized agency of the United Nations. It assists its 191 member countries in establishing international standards upon which national regulations are based, maintained by a Civil Aviation Authority (CAA).

In the United States, the Federal Aviation Administration (FAA) regulates air travel and aircraft operations. In Europe, a similar role is undertaken by the European Aviation Safety Agency, which formulates critical safety regulations governing airline operations.

Variation In Airline Regulations

Despite the ICAO's efforts towards standardization of airline regulations, these norms are still established at the national level, meaning that while member countries adhere to the same standards, the specifics of regulations can vary. Given that air travel is a complex and ever-evolving industry, regulations are subject to continuous changes and adaptations, making it crucial for those in the travel sector to stay abreast of the latest developments and news.

Airport Administration Overview

An airport authority is a Government organization that manages and supervises one or more airports. Typically, these authorities are guided by several airport commissioners appointed by a government official.

Aviation Auditors

An aviation auditor is responsible for ensuring a company's compliance with aviation regulations and other quality standards for quality Assurance. This ensures that the company adheres to legal guidelines and operates safely and efficiently. Auditing tasks may range from inspecting airport maintenance to reviewing financial data related to airplanes and airlines. Certifications from certifying bodies can open up additional career opportunities in this industry.

Duties and Responsibilities

Some aviation auditors provide internal auditing services within a company. Their role is to continuously monitor the company, regularly compiling reports on specific safety requirements and issues. When problems arise, they may suggest solutions such as enhanced training, policy revisions, or suspending unfit individuals.

Third-party aviation auditors are hired for impartial reviews of a company. They examine the company's processes and even scrutinize any internal audits to identify overlooked or deliberately omitted issues. Compliance checks include observing employees, reviewing manuals, and supervising training procedures.

In case of minor issues, an aviation auditor might collaborate with the company to address the problem. However, for significant security concerns, immediate actions, including a temporary halt of operations, may be necessary. If a company refuses to respond to an audit report, the auditor may be legally or ethically required to report the issue to a regulatory authority.

Aviation Inspector

Aviation inspectors play a critical role in ensuring the safety of air transport by reviewing all procedures, equipments and systems of an aircraft to ensure it meets all safety regulations as per the civil aviation

Duties and Responsibilities

Aviation inspectors perform a variety of duties to ensure the safe transportation of airline passengers. They investigate accidents and equipment malfunctions, inspect aircraft, air traffic controllers, navigation systems, and communication equipment, recommending necessary repairs. They review safety procedures and inspect maintenance practices to ensure airports and aircraft meet federal safety standards.

Aviation Instructor

Aviation instructors play a critical role in teaching students and air operators various aspects as guided by the 19 Aviation Annexes.

There are flight Instructors who teach students in Aviation Training Organisations and other ICAO certified instructors who train practising operators for compliance.

Aviation Industry is highly regulated and require continuous training making instructing one of the highly sought profession in Aviation.

Key Stakeholders in the Aviation Industry

a)Airlines, and Airline Owners

Owners of the airline, are the first and primary stakeholders.

b)Civil Aviation Authority

The state is the second key stakeholder, tasked with ensuring the safety, efficiency, and profitability of the country's air transportation system, including airlines.

c)Conssesionares

Suppliers such as labor, financial institutions, lessors, MROs, GDS, Travel Companies, Cargo Handling Agents, Freight Forwarding Agencies, and Airport and Aviation Service providers constitute the third group of stakeholders.

Government Agencies

The Government Agencies facilitate the passengers journey and cargo at various customer touch points i.e. port health, immigration, Customs and Security agencies to ensure safety and seamless service delivery.

d)Passengers

Lastly, the customers is the greatest stakeholder since all services and operations are aligned and dependant on their needs.

In conclusion, according to the International Air Transport Association's latest prediction, the African aviation industry is projected to grow to about 356 million passengers by 2038. The travel and tourism industry currently supports over 12 million jobs in the African region. As such, fostering stakeholder engagement and expanding air service are critical for driving regional economic development.

Operations Set-Up in the Aviation Industry: An In-Depth Look

Airport operations encompass a multitude of procedures that are designed to ensure that each passenger's journey through an airport runs seamlessly. With various departments such as customer support, Transportation Security Administration (TSA), and gate operators, it's crucial to have exceptional operational capabilities to deal with the thousands of travelers moving through an airport on a daily basis.

This sector presents a broad range of opportunities within the aviation industry. However, before delving into the various functions of aviation operations, it's critical to understand one vital stakeholder: the customer.

Understanding the Full Customer Experience at the Airport

The term 'customer experience' refers to the sum total of all the interactions a traveler has during their journey, effectively constituting their relationship with the airport. This includes experiences from the moment of departure, during layovers, and upon arrival at the destination airport. It could include interactions that occur in person, online, via self-service kiosks, or through other channels.

Each of these points of interaction, or 'touchpoints', contribute to defining moments - often termed 'moments of truth' that shape the overall customer experience. Properly managed, these touchpoints have the power to influence the customer's purchasing decisions and the potential for future business.

Applying the 'Peak-End' Theory to Customer Experience

The 'peak-end' rule posits that people judge an experience largely based on how they felt at its most intense point (the peak) and at its end. It means emotionally charged experiences tend to linger in memory longer than mundane ones. This is why airports should strive to provide emotionally enriching experiences that will create lasting memories and positively influence customers' perception.

However, it's crucial to understand that these peak moments may vary for different travelers, underscoring the importance of personalized customer experience management (CEM).

Creating a Customer Journey Map:

A customer journey map provides a visual representation of the entire customer experience, broken down into distinct phases that cover physical, digital, and social communication realms.

Phase 1: Attraction - This is the initial point of contact, where potential customers become aware of theservice, often through digital or social media channels.

Phase 2: Decision - At this point, customers decide whether to purchase the service. This decision-making process can involve digital platforms, phone conversations with call center agents, or physical stores that sell the service,

Phase 3: Purchase/Experience - This phase encompasses the actual purchase and the experience.

Phase 4: Support - This involves maintaining communication with customers before, during, and after the service, demonstrating support when things don't go as planned.

Phase 5: Retention - Airlines Service providers should strive to retain customers, particularly frequent consumers . This can be achieved through special offers, loyalty programs, and personalized communication.

Functions of Key Airport/Airline Operators

Role of a Flight Dispatcher

A Flight Dispatcher holds critical responsibilities in flight operations:

- Ensuring that the daily flight planning process is straightforward and secure.

- Providing the crew with optimal flight plans and the latest flight documentation.

- Offering comprehensive operational briefings to the crew.

- Supplying the most recent ATC flight plans to authorities and air traffic management.

- Confirming adherence to relevant regulations and operational procedures during flight planning.

- Making sure the flight planning aligns with operational manuals, current and forecasted weather conditions, and the operational readiness of critical en-route and terminal facilities.

Operations Control

An Operations Controller at the airport is responsible for:

- Ensuring the daily consistency of the company's flying schedule.

- Monitoring the fleet to ensure its safe and efficient operation.

- Confirming compliance with all relevant regulations and operational procedures.

- Maintaining an accurate and updated record of all aircraft's locations and technical status.

- Staying updated with current and forecasted weather conditions en route and the serviceability of critical en-route and terminal infrastructure affecting the route.

- Leading the response in the event of a flight disruption.

- Taking corrective measures in the event of a potential or actual disruption to maintain or restore the fleet to its original schedule.

Managing Air Cargo Operations

Air cargo management is one of the less recognized yet incredibly intricate facets of airport operations. It demands substantial industry knowledge and a broad array of technical skills to handle the varied internal and external challenges, as well as stakeholders. The roles and responsibilities in this domain can differ widely between facilities, akin to many other airport personnel functions.

The Air Cargo Manager plays a pivotal role in ensuring that all goods for delivery are in optimal condition. They oversee the cargo's transition from its temporary location (typically, an airplane) to the final recipient or user. The level of involvement may vary depending on the specifics of the operations and how the overall airport staff responsibilities have been distributed. However, one can reasonably expect an Air Cargo Manager to be proficient in various areas represented by the acronym PLOMS: Planning, Leasing and Property Development, Operations, Marketing, Stakeholder Outreach.

Duties of an Air Cargo Manager

An Air Cargo Manager is responsible for managing the transportation of their company's goods from the point of origin to the destination of the receiver. They maintain regular communication with the supply chain manager who tracks the freight that needs to be delivered, ensuring they are promptly informed in case of any delays. This facilitates effective communication with both the sender and the recipient.

Collaborating with various departments helps them stay updated about changes in schedules, limitations in freight space, and even customer requirements. The Air Cargo Manager ensures all freight and goods are manually counted, monitored, and recorded in a database. They also confirm that all freight is weighed and measured according to the airline's regulations.

When it comes to overnight storage, Air Cargo Managers ensure the cargo is stored in a reliable location and handled by professionals during loading and unloading. Additionally, they search for the best rates and airlines for freight forwarding, always striving to reduce freight costs by thoroughly researching all available airlines and their prices.

Working Environment

Air cargo management operates round the clock. As such, individuals interested in this field must be flexible with their work schedule

and ready to work extended hours if
necessary..

Untapped Potential in Africa's Aviation Industry: Opportunities in Freight Management

Global air cargo growth has been significantly
hindered by ongoing trade conflicts, notably
between the United States and China. Despite
this, the consumable or special cargo domain
has emerged as a beacon of resilience amidst
these challenging times. It is in this context that
the African air cargo market has stood out,
accounting for a substantial proportion of
perishable exports.

Further, Africa is currently undergoing a
notable digital transformation, and it is making
significant strides in the realms of
infrastructure development and liberalization.
These advancements are anticipated to boost
the African air freight sector, propelling it to
unprecedented heights.

Despite Africa only accounting for 2% of
global air freight, African carriers have,
according to the International Air Transport
Association (IATA), been expanding at a faster

pace than any other region for almost two years. This growth is partly due to strong commercial and investment ties with Asia, with capacity surging by 17.1% year on year, leading to a double-digit growth in air freight volumes between the two regions over the past year.

Investment - A Crucial Requirement for Africa

Dr. Olumuyiwa Benard Aliu,5th President of the International Civil Aviation Organization (ICAO), expressed that enhanced air connectivity in Africa and its associated promise of sustainable development will only materialize through the mobilization of sufficient and relevant investment.

As per ICAO's long-term traffic forecasts, both passenger and freight traffic in Africa are expected to grow annually by 4.3% and 3.8% respectively, until 2035. With Africa presently accounting for 4% of worldwide air transport services, it has the highest development potential among all of ICAO's geographic regions.

READY FOR TAKEOFF

African Airlines Paving the Way Forward

In May 2025, Kenya Airways the Pride of Africa co-hosted the first ever IATA Ground Handling Conference on African soil drawing over 1500+ delegates spotlighting operational modernization, work force development and airport- handler collaboration

Ethiopian Airlines at the APEX passenger Choice Award was voted the Best Overall in Africa.Ithas been pioneering capacity enhancement in the African air transport sector via a blend of airline acquisitions, strategic alliances, and significant investments. The airline is leveraging its expertise in other markets by collaborating with various governments to establish new national airlines, such as in Chad, and by acquiring non-controlling shares in other state-owned airlines, as seen in Zambia and Mozambique.

Kenya Airways in January 2024 marked a record high for the number of ebookings reinforcing an upward trend.As the industry continues to advance, ebooking is anticipated to enhance the efficiency and cost effectiveness of business and shaping the future of air cargo operations in the region.

In Conclusion

Sanjeev Gadhiya, CEO of Astral Aviation, posits that Africa's air cargo sector is on the brink of "extremely significant growth" in the coming years. This potential is bolstered by the commencement of the African Continental Free Trade Area (AfCFTA) and new open markets that have emerged in the wake of the pandemic.

Gadhiya noted that the suspension of various transport services during the COVID-19 crisis amplified the demand for cargo flights, which in turn, projected to aid African airlines in reaching greater heights than ever before.

LESSON 4:

Exercising Leadership In The Aviation Industry

Introduction: Leading in a High-Stakes Environment

Aviation is one of the most complex industries in the world. Every day, thousands of people from pilots and cabin crew to regulators and engineers depend on leadership to keep systems safe and efficient. Leadership in aviation isn't confined to CEOs or directors; it emerges at every level, from air traffic control to cabin crew. This lesson explores what effective leadership looks like in aviation and how you can develop it.

Deep Dive: Dimensions of Aviation Leadership

1. **Regulatory Leadership:** Civil Aviation Authorities (CAAs) enforce ICAO standards and keep skies safe.

2. **Corporate Leadership:** Airline and airport executives drive investment, innovation, and customer trust.
3. **Operational Leadership:** Duty managers, flight dispatchers, and crew leaders ensure daily smooth operations.
4. **Crisis Leadership:** Leaders must respond to pandemics, hijackings, IT failures, and weather disruptions with calm and clarity.
5. **Ethical Leadership:** Integrity and accountability are critical in an industry where errors can cost lives.

Case Study: During the COVID-19 pandemic, *Kenya Airways* leaders pivoted toward cargo when passenger demand collapsed. This agile leadership kept the airline profitable while others grounded fleets.

Exercises

1. **Leader Profile:** Choose one aviation leader (past or present). Write a short biography of their leadership style and impact.

2. **Crisis Drill:** Imagine you are an airport manager during a fuel shortage. Draft a 1-page leadership plan to keep operations safe and passengers informed.

3. **Self-Assessment:** Score yourself (1–10) on decision-making, communication, adaptability, and empathy. Identify the skill you most need to improve.

Action Framework: Becoming an Aviation Leader

1. **Study Governance:** Learn how ICAO, IATA, and national CAAs influence aviation policy.

2. **Practice Leadership:** Take small leadership roles in student groups, clubs, or community projects.

3. **Master Communication:** Enroll in public speaking or negotiation training.

4. **Live Integrity:** Commit to ethical decision-making in all situations.

5. **Seek Mentorship:** Find a leader in aviation to guide your career journey.

Reflection Journal

- Who is one aviation leader I admire, and why?
- How do I personally react under pressure and how can I improve?
- What small leadership role can I take now to prepare for greater responsibilities later?

CHAPTER FIVE

HUMAN RESOURCES IN THE AVIATION INDUSTRY: CRITICAL ISSUES AND OPPORTUNITIES

THE SURGE IN AFRICA'S aviation industry has brought with it a demanding challenge: the lack of sufficient human resources in civil aviation. This issue directly impacts the availability of trained technical aviation personnel and the ability of African countries to effectively implement ICAO Standards and Recommended Practices (SARPs) and other initiatives by ICAO.

Consequently, there is an urgent need to bolster the competency of the African civil aviation sector and enhance the skills of its human resources. Recognizing the gravity of this matter, High-level Ministerial Segment endorsed the Doha Ministerial Declaration on enhancing Human resource and training during the ICAO Facilitation Conference (FALC2025) in April 2025.The outcome is reflected in Annex 9 updates and 2025 ICAO Assembly.

Labor Relations in the Aviation Industry

The aviation industry has three key characteristics which make labor relations a critical concern. Firstly, the industry's product is perishable, with airlines lacking a tangible inventory. If flights are delayed, airlines can neither "stockpile" nor swiftly recuperate lost traffic.

Secondly, air travel demand is pro-cyclical, intensifying or shrinking in response to economic growth or decline, but at a markedly higher rate. Economic fluctuations significantly impact airline revenues and profits, particularly regarding business class flights.

Thirdly, labor comprises a large portion of total operational costs and is one of the few variable costs under direct managerial control, unlike costs like fuel, landing charges, and aircraft costs. Labor expenses typically constitute a fifth of Asian airlines' total costs and a third of costs incurred by European and American airlines. In sectors such as air traffic control, labor costs account for nearly two-thirds of operating expenses. These characteristics significantly influence human resource policies and labor relations in the industry.

Impact of Perishability and Economic Conditions on Employment

Owing to the "perishability factor", airlines will aim to rapidly cut down capacity in crisis situations to mitigate financial losses. This leads to both direct and indirect job losses, including jobs at the airline in question and jobs in various support activities like catering, cleaning, fueling, airport services, local suppliers, and more. Research suggests that for every single job lost by an airline, four to ten jobs are lost within the airport's periphery, with a minimum of three jobs lost outside the airport's boundaries.

This pattern of job loss often reveals a misalignment between management and labor objectives in accordance with current or future market conditions. In a recession or crisis, airlines experience a higher drop in demand than most associated businesses, and costs need to be tightly controlled. Employees are often required to make sacrifices to safeguard the airline's financial condition. However, during times of economic growth, employees expect their pay and benefits to rise in line with the company's prosperity.

The COVID-19 Crisis and the Aviation Industry

The outbreak of COVID-19 and the ensuing global health crisis had profound implications for the aviation industry. Borders and airspace were closed to prevent the spread of the virus, causing an unprecedented economic crisis in the industry.

According to data from the International Air Transport Association (IATA), global air passenger demand (measured by global revenue passenger kilometers) saw a significant drop in the first quarter of 2020 (52.9% less than in 2019). The lockdowns also severely disrupted the industrial cargo sector due to a drop in production and compromised supply chain.

While the transportation of medical supplies provided some reprieve for the freight sector, regional and global air travel took heavy losses, with airlines losing about half of their value.

The Aviation Industry in the Post-Pandemic Era

The devastating impact of the COVID-19 pandemic on the aviation industry is indisputable. With government-imposed lockdowns and travel bans, jobs were lost across the industry, from pilots and crew to ground staff. Despite proposals for aviation bailout measures, airlines were compelled to trim down their expenses to stay afloat. The United Nations World Travel Organization reported a staggering drop in foreign tourism, by 60-80% in 2020.

As the world adjusted to the reality of the pandemic, the aviation industry adopted new norms and protocols which calls for innovational approach. This has created numerous job and business opportunities in the Aviation Industry ranging from new technology and innovative approach to business.

The Value of Human Resources in the Aviation Industry

In an industry as strategically important as aviation, human resource management (HRM), particularly employee training, is a crucial yet often overlooked area. The focus on passenger health and safety, highlighted especially after 9/11, underscored the value of ground and crew training programs.

HRM, which is closely linked to individual and organizational growth, necessitates policies and procedures across multiple systems, such as recruitment and screening for the acquisition of skilled staff, to meet corporate and customer needs. HRM plays a vital role in framing the organization's objectives and effectively communicating them to employees, thus contributing to their professional development.

Africa: A Rising Power in Aviation

The African continent boasts the world's youngest and fastest-growing population, with more than 60% of its 1.2 billion people under 25 years old. The population of its 55 nations is projected to more than double by 2055. Africa, with over 400 million young people, holds the promise of a massive human capacity that needs to be effectively harnessed. This burgeoning population, backed by a growing industrial sector, views aviation as a key driver of socio-economic development. The industry supports over 12 million jobs and contributes more than $ 65 billion in GDP.

The Role of African Governments in Aviation

Governments across Africa are grappling with the challenge of expanding the continent's air transport potential through new and modernized infrastructure. Efforts have been made, with ICAO's support, to increase youth participation in the promising future of aviation careers. The Next Generation of

Aviation Proffessionals(NGAP) is a critical global program with deep significance for the future of aviation.

Given an industry so reliant on talent management and employee engagement, the shift in focus to human capital is understandable.By 2036, ICAO project a need for 620,000 new pilots, 125,000new air traffic controllers, 1.3 million aircraft maintenance personnel among other key areas.

Mentorship Programs in the African Aviation Industry

For many young professionals eager to succeed but unsure where to begin, mentorship can be a vital tool. Mentors can help set realistic goals and assign appropriate tasks. Accepting responsibilities that offer growth opportunities often marks the first step towards professional and career success.

The aviation industry offers a plethora of technical and well-paying jobs that demand a solid educational background and on-the-job experience. Mentors can serve as invaluable resources for individuals starting or growing their careers in a vibrant industry with diverse career options. With many aviation specialists on the cusp of retirement, guiding young professionals through their professional growth in the sector is beneficial to them and crucial for the aviation community to cultivate a robust cadre of future leaders and officials.

In the quest for mentors, it's crucial to look both within and outside the industry. Progressive companies are committed to building a successful mentoring program within their own organizations, and providing employees with additional channels for mentorship and communication in the sector.

Internal mentors can offer insight into the company culture, as well as career development opportunities and advancement. They are vested in the success of your company. On the other hand, external mentors can provide a broader perspective, impartial advice, and assistance in carving out a successful career path. They are more likely to help you navigate internal company issues that you might feel uncomfortable discussing with internal mentors.

Finding a Mentor and the Importance of Networking

Despite the importance of mentorship in specialized industries, finding the right mentor can be challenging. The process can be organic, stemming from 'on-the-job' interactions with colleagues, or facilitated by companies and industry groups. Both approaches are beneficial for mentor development and often result in a variety of opportunities for individuals new to the field.

The importance of networking cannot be overstated. Fortunately, a novice professional can join various groups and organizations to connect with key industry leaders and influencers. To gain a mentor in the aviation industry, it's important to interact with young professionals, spend time with them, and make an effort to connect with peers at professional conferences, exhibit halls, networking events, community events, and other major industry events.

Case in Point: YACAfrica(Young Aviation Club of Africa

The Young Aviators Club of Africa (YACAfrica) founded by Captain Mercy Makau is rapidly growing into one of the most influential platform for nurturing the next generation of aviation and aerospace proffessionals in Africa.The club with over 60,000 members is engaged in industry exposure for youth, innovation & research,drone training, aviation camps,community outreach & advocacy, mentorship and leadership development among other programs.

Conclusion

The resurgence of African aviation following the Covid 19 pandemic brought numerous opportunities for innovation and paradime shift from manual way of doing things to AI and much more. The sky is limitless for the African Aviation Industry. If they can seize this new blend of realigned business strategies, streamlined regulations, and strategic collaborations, especially as the African Continental Free Trade Agreement (AfCFTA) enhances intra-African trade and travel opportunities to unprecedented heights, there's nothing to prevent them from realizing their true potential.

LESSON 5:

Human Resources In Aviation

Introduction: People Are the True Engines of Aviation

Aircraft may dominate the skies, but it is people who keep aviation moving. From engineers and technicians to cabin crew and customer service agents, human resources (HR) is at the heart of every successful airline or airport. In Africa, where aviation is growing but faces a shortage of skilled professionals, HR challenges and opportunities are especially critical. This lesson explores how people power the industry and how you can position yourself in this vital space.

Deep Dive: HR Challenges and Opportunities in Aviation

1. **Talent Shortages:** By 2036, the world will need **620,000 new pilots** and **1.3 million technicians**. Africa must prepare to fill its share.

2. **Training Gaps:** Many African students must study abroad due to limited local aviation academies. Expanding training capacity is vital.

3. **Mentorship & Knowledge Transfer:** With senior professionals nearing retirement, mentoring young talent is critical to avoid brain drain.

4. **Labor Relations:** Strikes and disputes highlight the need for fair HR policies and worker engagement.

5. **Post-Pandemic Shifts:** COVID-19 created demand for digital skills, resilience, and flexible work systems.

Case Study: *The Young Aviators Club of Africa (YACAfrica),* led by Captain Mercy Makau, has over 60,000 members. Through camps, mentorship, and drone training, it shows how grassroots HR initiatives can shape the future workforce.

Exercises

1. **Skills Gap Check:** Write down three aviation roles you're interested in.

Research the required skills. Which ones do you already have? Which must you build?

2. **Mentorship Plan:** Identify two potential mentors (local or global). Draft a short introduction you could send to request mentorship.

3. **HR Challenge Roleplay:** Imagine you're an HR manager resolving a strike by Airport security staff. Write a half-page strategy to address concerns and maintain operations.

Action Framework: Building Aviation Talent

1. **Commit to Learning:** Explore ICAO, IATA, or local aviation authority training opportunities.

2. **Seek Mentorship:** Join programs or associations that connect young professionals with senior leaders.

3. **Promote Skills Development:** Focus on both technical training and soft skills (communication, teamwork).

4. **Support Local Growth:** Advocate for government and private investment in aviation training centers in Africa.
5. **Adapt to the Future:** Explore HR technology like e-learning platforms, digital recruitment, and AI workforce planning.

Reflection Journal

- What aviation role excites me most, and what training path leads there?
- Do I have a mentor today? If not, who could I approach?
- How can I contribute to strengthening aviation talent in my country?

CHAPTER SIX

MARKETING OPPORTUNITIES IN AVIATION

IN THE HIGHLY COMPETITIVE and dynamic landscape of the aviation industry, marketing holds a pivotal role. It operates as the driving force behind brand identity, customer reach, and ultimately, business growth. The importance of marketing in the aviation sector cannot be understated. It is the key ingredient that bridges the gap between the Aviation service offerings and the customers it seeks to attract and retain.

Importance of Marketing in the Aviation Sector

Effective marketing campaigns and strategies enable operators to establish a strong brand identity. It's not just about offering services and goods; it's about crafting a narrative that resonates with the target audience. The brand identity communicates the operator's vision, mission, values, and promise to its customers, influencing their perception and choice.

In an industry where service offerings may seem homogeneous, marketing provides an opportunity for differentiation. Through creative and innovative marketing campaigns, operators can distinguish themselves from competitors, highlighting unique features, services, or pricing structures that make them an attractive choice for travelers.

Marketing plays a crucial role in both attracting new customers and retaining existing ones. Strategic marketing initiatives help raise brand awareness, persuade potential customers to choose theservice provider, and nurture relationships with existing customers to foster loyalty. The end goal is not only to sell but also to build a community of loyal customers who prefer the brand over all others.

Evolving Trends in Aviation Marketing

In the digital age, marketing trends in the aviation industry are continuously evolving. Keeping pace with these changes is critical for airport operators to maintain relevance and competitive edge.

Today, the majority of travelers are digital natives, which has led to a shift in marketing strategies towards online platforms. Social media, in particular, has become a powerful tool formarketing, allowing them to engage directly with their customers, respond to queries in real-time, and foster a sense of community.

More than ever before, operators are focusing on improving the customer experience. This approach has redefined marketing strategies, shifting them from a primarily sales-driven approach to one that puts customer satisfaction at the forefront.

As consumers become increasingly aware of their environmental impact, Airports are adopting green initiatives, not only in their operations but also in their marketing strategies. They are promoting their efforts towards reducing carbon emissions, eliminating single-use plastics, and more. This alignment of marketing strategies with sustainable practices helps attract environmentally conscious customers and builds a positive brand image.

In conclusion, the success of any service provider in today's competitive landscape hinges significantly on its marketing strategies. Understanding the current trends and incorporating them effectively is key to maintaining a strong presence in the aviation industry.

The Integral Role of Customer Service in the Aviation Sector

Customer service in the aviation sector forms the backbone of the industry's operations. It directly influences the passenger's overall travel experience, shaping their perception of the Airport and determining their likelihood of future engagements with the brand. Given the high-stakes nature of air travel, the provision of high-quality customer service becomes an even more crucial factor in this industry.

Detailed Overview of Customer Service in Aviation

Definition and Scope: Customer service in aviation refers to all the interactions and services that are provided to thepassengersthroughout their journey. This covers a wide array of touchpoints, ranging from ground transport, availability of basic services, screening services, booking and check-in processes, shopping services at the lounges to in-flight services and handling of grievances and complaints.

Importance of Customer Service: Quality customer service in aviation goes a long way in fostering customer loyalty and driving customer satisfaction. It can turn a one-time passenger into a regular flyer, contributing significantly to revenue increase. Furthermore, positive customer experiences shared via word-of-mouth or social media can boost reputation and attract new customers.

Challenges Faced by the Industry in Providing Effective Customer Service

Operational Challenges: Given the complex nature of aviation operations, operators often struggle with maintaining punctuality and managing unexpected circumstances like flight delays or cancellations, which can impact customer satisfaction.

Diverse Customer Needs: Each passenger has unique needs and expectations, which makes it challenging for operators to provide personalized service on a mass scale.

High-Pressure Environment: The fast-paced, high-stakes nature of air travel can lead to tense situations where excellent customer service becomes even more critical but also more challenging to deliver.

Strategies to Overcome these Challenges and Improve Customer Service

Technological Advancements: operators are increasingly leveraging technology to improve their customer service. This includes self-service kiosks for quicker check-ins, mobile apps for easy booking and real-time updates, in-flight entertainment systems, and AI-powered chatbots for round-the-clock customer support.

Staff Training: operators invest heavily in customer service training for their staff to ensure they can handle a variety of situations professionally and courteously. This includes training for effective communication, problem-solving, and stress management.

Personalization: To cater to diverse customer needs, airlines are focusing on providing personalized services. This could range from personalized meal options to seat preferences or special assistance for those in need.

Proactive Communication: To mitigate the impact of operational challenges on customer satisfaction, operators strive to keep their passengers informed. This includes proactive communication about flight delays, cancellations, or changes in boarding gates via SMS, email, or mobile app notifications.

By focusing on these strategies, operators can navigate the complexities of providing customer service in the aviation sector, ultimately leading to enhanced customer satisfaction and loyalty.

Understanding Customer Behavior in Aviation

Understanding customer behavior is key to any successful business, and aviation is no exception. The manner in which passengers make decisions, from selecting an airline to evaluating their travel experience, directly influences an airline's strategy to enhance customer satisfaction and loyalty.

An Overview of the Typical Aviation Customer Profile

Demographics and Preferences: The aviation customer base is diverse, ranging from business travelers and leisure tourists to students studying abroad and families on holiday. Each demographic has unique needs and preferences. For example, business travelers may prioritize punctuality and in-flight productivity tools, while leisure tourists may value budget-friendly options and in-flight comfort.

Travel Purpose: The reason for travel also significantly affects a customer's behavior. For instance, those traveling for business might be less price-sensitive but more concerned about flight schedules and reliability.

Behavior Patterns: Aviation customers also exhibit patterns in booking behavior, such as making reservations well in advance for planned vacations or opting for last-minute bookings for urgent business trips. Recognizing these patterns can help airlines/airports tailor their offerings and services to better meet their customers' needs.

Addressing Customer Complaints

Effective complaint handling is a cornerstone of superior customer service. By addressing complaints appropriately and promptly, operators not only resolve immediate issues but also build a stronger relationship with their customers.

Detailed Exploration of the Nature of Customer Complaints in Aviation

Types of Complaints: Complaints in the aviation sector may arise from a wide range of issues, such as delayed or canceled flights, lost or damaged luggage, poor in-flight services, or unprofessional behavior from staff. Each type of complaint necessitates a different response and resolution strategy.

Underlying Factors: Behind every complaint lies a gap between customer expectations and the actual service delivered. These expectations may relate to flight punctuality, comfort, food quality, luggage safety, or staff behavior. Understanding these underlying factors is crucial for preventing future complaints.

Importance of Effective Complaint Handling and Its Impact on Customer Loyalty

Restoring Trust: When operator air operator address complaints effectively, they can restore the damaged trust and potentially turn dissatisfied customers into loyal ones.

Continuous Improvement: Complaints provide valuable feedback for operator to improve their services. By identifying common issues in complaints, they can target specific areas for enhancement.

Reputation Management: Effective complaint handling can mitigate the negative impact of service failures on an operator's reputation. In contrast, poorly handled complaints can spread quickly in the age of social media, causing significant damage to the image.

Effective complaint handling requires a thorough understanding of the nature of complaints and the implementation of effective resolution strategies. By handling complaints properly, operators can increase customer satisfaction,s00 foster loyalty, and enhance their reputation in the competitive aviation industry.

V. Strategies for Resolving Customer Complaints

The ability to resolve customer complaints effectively is a critical skill in the aviation sector. By employing best practices, operator air operators can not only address individual issues but also enhance overall customer satisfaction and loyalty.

Comprehensive Guide to Best Practices for Complaint Resolution

Listening Actively: This is the first and perhaps most crucial step in complaint resolution. Understand the customer's perspective and their concerns. This step conveys to the customer that the air operator values their feedback and is committed to resolving the issue.

Empathy: Empathy is a powerful tool in complaint resolution. It helps in defusing tension and assures the customer that their feelings are understood.

Offering Solutions: Once the issue is understood, provide a solution. The resolution should not just be a quick fix but should also prevent the problem from recurring in the future.

Following Up: After providing a solution, follow up with the customer to ensure their issue has been fully resolved. This follow-up reaffirms the airline's commitment to customer satisfaction.

Meeting and Exceeding Customer Needs

In a highly competitive industry like aviation, merely meeting customer expectations is often not enough; exceeding them is the key to gaining an edge over competitors. This chapter dives into the importance of understanding and surpassing customer needs, along with the strategies and innovations operators use to achieve this.

Importance of Meeting Customer Needs for Customer Retention

Customer retention is crucial to the profitability and long-term success of any business, and the aviation sector is no exception. When operators successfully meet their customers' needs, they build a loyal customer base that often results in repeat business, positive word-of-mouth advertising, and higher profit margins.

Customer Loyalty: Meeting customer needs fosters loyalty. Loyal customers are more likely to stay with a particular operator and less likely to be swayed by competitors.

Word-of-Mouth Advertising: Satisfied customers tend to share their positive experiences with others, which can be a powerful marketing tool.

Profitability: Retaining existing customers is often more cost-effective than acquiring new ones, leading to increased profitability.

International Customer Satisfaction Survey – ACI

The ACI's Airport Service Quality (ASQ) customer satisfaction barometer is not a methodology but a visual dashboard representation of key results from the ASQ Departures survey data collected quarterly from participating airports.

The barometer displays a variety of overall scores and other totals, such as by category, region, and airport size. This barometer report is published quarterly, with a more detailed annual report presenting general customer satisfaction scores per Passenger Personas, which are classifications of customers/passengers sharing similar characteristics and attitudes.

The barometer's primary goal is to provide a global snapshot of overall satisfaction scores at the global and regional level, enabling airports worldwide to benchmark themselves against their peers.

Marketing jobs Available in the Aviation Space

Branding specialists – Their role is to maintain the organization's image and develop branding strategy.

Digital Marketing Specialist – They handle online campaigns, social media and advitisements.

Product Marketing specialists – Works on marketing for services and products for the organization,

Loyalty programs specialist – manages and develops programs for frequent and repeat customers for retention.

Passenger Experience specialist – Focuses on improving the customers'journey for value addition.

Events and partnership coordinator – Organizes promotions, expos and campains for customer attraction.

Technical Marketing Analyst – Combines technology insight with sales and product marketing.

Business Development specialist – Attracts logistic clients and builds brand presence.

Market Intelligence Analyst – Tracks demand, pricing, and competitor trends in logistics..

Content Creator – Develops aviation-relevant articles, newsletters and social media content.

Customer complaints expert – Handles customer feedback .

Communication expert – communicates/Promotes aviation policies, safety campaigns and innovation initiatives

The opportunities require open attitudes to innovation and exploration.

Conclusion

As we conclude our exploration of marketing in the aviation industry, it's crucial to reflect on the key themes that have emerged throughout this chapter.

Marketing in the aviation sector plays a crucial role in fostering customer satisfaction, loyalty, and business success. Understanding the integral role of customer service in the aviation industry sets the foundation for this, with a focus on recognizing and overcoming challenges to improve customer experiences.

Delving into customer behavior, we have seen that understanding your audience is pivotal to delivering a service that meets and exceeds their expectations. Identifying customer complaints and resolving them effectively helps in maintaining high levels of customer loyalty, ultimately leading to a stronger brand reputation and healthier profit margins.

The role of digital marketing, personalization, proactive service, and innovative offerings all contribute to a richer and more rewarding customer experience.

As we look towards the future, the aviation sector is poised for even more significant changes and advancements. With the acceleration of digital transformations and technological advancements, we can anticipate more personalized, efficient, and customer-centric services.

In summary, the future of marketing in the aviation sector will be about balancing technological advancements with a continued focus on customer satisfaction and sustainable practices.

LESSON 6:

Marketing Opportunities In Aviation

Introduction: Selling the Skies

In aviation, marketing is more than flashy ads or billboards it's the art of shaping perception, building trust, and creating loyalty. Airlines and airports don't just sell seats or gates; they sell **experiences**. In Africa, where competition is intensifying and new players are entering the market, smart marketing can mean the difference between stagnation and success.

Deep Dive: The Power of Aviation Marketing

1. **Brand Identity:** Every airline projects an image luxury (Emirates), affordability (Ryanair), or connectivity (Ethiopian). Africa's carriers must craft clear stories.
2. **Customer Experience (CX):** Marketing lives in every touchpoint from online booking to baggage delivery and in-flight service.

3. **Digital Marketing:** Social media, influencer campaigns, and mobile-first tools are critical for today's digital traveler.
4. **Sustainability as Strategy:** Travelers increasingly choose airlines based on eco-friendly policies like carbon offsetting or biofuel use.
5. **Tourism Integration:** Airlines can partner with tourism boards, hotels, and local businesses to market destinations not just flights.

Case Study: *Kenya Airways* branded itself as the "Pride of Africa." Through cultural storytelling, sponsorships, and regional partnerships, it built global recognition even while navigating financial challenges.

Exercises

1. **Brand Audit:** Pick one African airline. List its three strongest marketing strengths and two weaknesses.

2. **Social Media Campaign:** Draft three short posts that could attract more young travelers to fly with a local airline.
3. **Customer Journey Map:** Trace your steps from booking a ticket to arriving at your destination. Where could marketing improve your experience?

Action Framework: Building Aviation Marketing Skills

1. **Study Customer Psychology:** Learn what drives loyalty comfort, price, reliability, or brand image.
2. **Go Digital:** Practice with tools like social media ads, SEO, and Google Analytics.
3. **Specialize in CX:** Enroll in customer service management or CX training.
4. **Think Green:** Promote sustainability as part of your brand strategy.
5. **Explore Consulting:** Aviation marketing consultants can work with airlines, airports, or tourism boards.

Reflection Journal

- Which airline's brand do I admire most, and why?
- How can African airlines use marketing to compete with global carriers?
- If I created a campaign for an airline today, what message would I emphasize?

CHAPTER SEVEN

TECHNOLOGICAL AVENUES IN AVIATION

IN INDUSTRIES LIKE AVIATION aviation, data communication and technology play an integral role, as it's now easier and more straightforward to access information using technology.

The advent of technology has been pivotal in increasing the operational efficiency of air operators. Through sophisticated technology and IT advancements, air operators have managed to reduce costs and improve processes. Technology has facilitated better networks and a superior travel experience for passengers. For instance, Visa processing, baggage tracking, security screening among others.

The information technology transformation since 2020 has proven to be a game-changer. It can enable the aviation industry to prioritize efficiency and reliability while reducing costs. In some areas, operators compete with each other in technology, while in others, technology serves the shared interests of these aviation businesses.

As the pace of technological change is rapid, strategizing for air operators becomes complex and challenging. As the tech sector advances faster than other industries can keep pace with, issues like data security become increasingly challenging to address.

Contributions Of Information Technology To The Aviation Industry

The use of social CRM (customer relationship management) has made a significant contribution, as it has proven to be a critical element in customer relationship management. Platforms like Twitter, tiktok and Facebook have created new avenues for businesses to interact with their customers and build loyalty.

Many operators are also looking to install new technological equipment for passenger comfort, such as automated services reducing human interventions and bottle necks, .

Another example of a technological contribution to the aviation sector is navigation technology.

An essential aspect of technology is highly secure software to protect both the organization's and the passenger's private data.

Airport Departure Control System

The departure control system (DCS) is a multi-host system or technology used for computerized check-ins, boarding, and load control. It is available from various providers and has proven to be robust. A DCS is functionally rich and has demonstrated its versatility on a wide range of models and crafts.

A DCS also supports the alliance network as well as the priority component of passenger handling. It focuses not only on airline procedures at the airport but also on administrative requirements such as immigration and customs.

Airport Check-In Via the Internet

Computers, tablets, or smartphones can be used by passengers to check airlines' websites. Thus, passengers can conveniently book a seat and save or print their tickets, all from their own home or office. If there is no need for or requirement for baggage check-in, the passenger can go directly to the governmental procedures.

Maintenance of Aircraft

Aircraft provide a fast, safe, and comfortable means of transportation, and the aviation industry as a whole is changing the way people travel. But it requires a considerable amount of expertise to build and maintain an aircraft.

A team of aviation maintenance specialists is responsible for maintaining commercial planes. Air control, pressure checks, lifts, and aerodynamics are some technologies that aid in the maintenance and flight of an aircraft.

Innovation provides the necessary fuel for aviation to help humans fly faster, higher, cheaper, and better than ever before. Furthermore, technological advancements assist the physics of aviation dynamics in developing better aviation vehicles, such as civilian planes, fighter planes, and cargo planes, all of which are built for different purposes.

Technological advances and innovations have made it possible for the general public to travel around the world without incurring significant financial costs.

Digitizing and Modern Travel Technologies in the Aviation Industry

Digital innovation, an economic version of the Internet of Things (IoT), connects smart machines, technical analyses, and humans. Sensors collect information for code review and decision-making. Air operators around the world are making strides toward their digital transformation goals by investing in cloud storage, data centers, Wi-Fi onboard staff services, and autonomous data processing. These are all fundamental elements in achieving digitized flight operations.

The Digital Revolution also known as the Third Industrial Revolution is at a tipping point, impacting traditional industries like energy, manufacturing, and aviation. According to experts in these fields, sensors, machinery, and IT tools can all be linked to analyze information, leading to faster, more adaptable, and more efficient processes. However, many of these executives are still unsure how digital technologies can assist them in achieving strategic objectives.

Various airports are now improving passenger experiences with digital innovations and amenities. Airline digital Business Process Management (BPM) is responsible for managing business processes affected by digital transformation. BPM practices are essential for improving customer satisfaction.

Flight's Digitization

Several advanced airline software and services offer key strategic breakthroughs that provide airlines with immediate future benefits in daily air operations. Airlines can enhance their overall operations by assisting with tasks associated with each stage of the journey.

As a result of digitization, cockpit functions have become increasingly automated. Pilots now have access to a networked environment of applications, tools, and reports that outline the future flight deck. Thanks to specialized applications, pilots can access a wealth of valuable information from a single handheld device.

Going digital significantly reduces pilots' workload. For example, the ability to digitally transfer briefings or submit reports via a device that connects at the gate decreases paperwork. Digitization also improves efficiency and productivity. Consider specialized apps that provide current weather information, for instance. These apps offer graphically enhanced views of market-leading meteorological data, enabling more adaptable and responsive operations, safer and more cost-effective flight paths.

Establishing a unified digital platform for aircraft application testing also simplifies interactions between pilots and ground-based staff. Many have had to adapt to remote work. Similarly, implementing a digital app suite for crew members allows them to focus more on customer service while reducing administrative costs.

Blockchain Technology

The aviation industry can use blockchain technology in several ways to improve operational efficiency, security, and customer experience. For example:

Airlines can eliminate the need for physical ID verifications by storing passenger information in a decentralized virtual database accessible by relevant personnel, using blockchain technology.

Blockchain technology can be incredibly useful in developing a secure data management system for customers.

Virtual Reality and Augmented Reality

The AR/VR revolution is being used in various industries, including retail and healthcare. The airline sector is following suit. One of the most apparent uses of these technologies is expected to be seen in the airport space, where AR/VR-based applications can be employed for an enhanced airport experience.

Biometrics

The Aviation industry is continuously striving to enhance passengers' travel experiences. One such initiative is the implementation of biometrics technology at airline and airport touchpoints. The concept of biometrics was introduced with the "Happy Flow" project in 2015. This project aimed to make a seamless and secure flying process possible. Recently, numerous biometric-enabled single token platforms have been developed, and airlines and airports are using them to transform passenger experiences.

Aviation Digital Opportunities for Young Professionals

Throughout the 20th and the early 21st centuries, various crises and events have driven innovation. The COVID-19 pandemic swept across national borders in early 2020, wreaking havoc on economies and social structures in both developed and developing nations. A wide range of industries have been affected, and the aviation sector, a significant contributor to global economic growth, has not been exempt.

However, due to its adaptability and receptiveness to innovation and development, business aviation is a trendsetter within the entire aerospace sector, continuously pushing novel ideas and solutions forward.

Airports Are Becoming More Digital

Touchless Technology at Airports

The expansion and development of touchless systems at airports is another innovation. Given the virus's ability to spread via surface contact, cleaning touchpoints is essential. Implementing new protocols and practices across all airport operations to reduce close contact can help airlines reassure passengers of their safety and wellbeing.

Check-In With Biometrics

The accelerated adoption of biometric technologies is an example of a positive effect of COVID-19. Biometric boarding involves using facial recognition to verify passenger identity at airports.

There has been talk of a generational shift in commercial aviation for more than a decade. As the average age of managers in the industry rises, experts have provided guidance on how to recruit, educate, and integrate young people into teams and understand what they require as consumers.

The next generation is now coming of age. Young leaders and entrepreneurs under the age of 40 are carving out a space in the industry, and they have unique insights into the future of commercial aviation. Young professionals in the sector can help advance these trends and make improvements. By bolstering internal processes with diverse technological tools, they can help companies adapt to new, more efficient, and innovative ways of working, especially in the short term. They can have a lasting impact on the world by making business travel more efficient and sustainable.

Conclusion

Digitalization has been instrumental in enhancing airline operational efficiency. It helps the aviation industry maximize the potential of its technologies and platforms. It also facilitates the adoption and evolution of global standards and provides value to companies.

Innovations inspired by COVID-19 are examined in terms of their nature and behavior. A range of operational and product enhancements inspired by COVID-19 have been implemented in response to the crisis. Despite the disruption of established routines and systems, the threat to the existence of several major airlines seems to have encouraged employees to embrace innovation.

LESSON 7:

Technology & Innovation In Aviation

Introduction: Flying Into the Digital Future

Aviation has always been driven by technology from the Wright brothers' first powered flight to today's AI-assisted cockpits and touchless airports. In the 21st century, technology is no longer just about engines and wings; it's about **data, connectivity, and digital transformation**. For Africa, where infrastructure gaps persist, technology offers a chance to **leapfrog**, adopting drones, biometrics, AI, and blockchain earlier than older markets.

Deep Dive: Game-Changing Technologies

1. **Digitalization & Automation:** Cloud storage, IoT, digital crew apps, and automated check-in reduce costs and streamline passenger journeys.
2. **Drones & UAVs:** Delivering blood, medicines, and agricultural products in

countries like Rwanda and Ghana, proving drones are more than gadgets they're lifesavers.

3. **Biometrics & Touchless Travel:** From "Happy Flow" single-token platforms to airport facial recognition, biometrics are redefining convenience and safety.

4. **Blockchain:** Strengthens data security, ticketing systems, and passenger ID management while reducing fraud.

5. **VR/AR & Simulation:** Enhancing pilot training, airport design, and passenger experience with immersive technologies.

6. **Green Tech:** Biofuels, hybrid engines, and lightweight materials are key to cutting aviation's carbon footprint.

Case Study: *Zipline* pioneered medical drone delivery in Rwanda, scaling operations during COVID-19 to deliver millions of vaccines. Its success shows how combining **regulatory openness** with innovative tech can make Africa a global aviation leader.

Exercises

1. **Tech Scan:** Pick one technology (AI, drones, biometrics, blockchain). Write a one-page report on how it is being applied in Africa today.
2. **Innovation Idea:** Imagine you are a startup founder using drones in agriculture, logistics, or healthcare. Draft your 200-word concept pitch.
3. **Skills Match:** List two of your personal skills (e.g., coding, design, project management). Brainstorm how they could contribute to aviation tech.

Action Framework: Becoming a Tech-Savvy Aviation Professional

1. **Upskill Continuously:** Explore short courses on AI, drones, and aviation IT systems (e.g., ICAO e-learning, Coursera).
2. **Stay Updated:** Follow IATA, ICAO, and African aviation innovation labs for the latest trends.

3. **Start Local Projects:** Join a drone club, build a small aviation app, or experiment with IoT solutions.
4. **Network in Tech Circles:** Connect with aviation startups like Astral Aviation (cargo drones) or Zipline.
5. **Think Sustainability:** Focus on green aviation technologies that reduce emissions and waste.

Reflection Journal

- Which aviation technology excites me the most, and why?
- How can Africa use technology to leapfrog traditional barriers to aviation growth?
- What is one skill I can build in the next 6 months to make me more valuable in aviation's digital future?

CHAPTER TEN

HIGHLIGHTS ON THE SECTORS SHAPING THE ECONOMIC LANDSCAPE OF THE AVIATION INDUSTRY

THE AVIATION INDUSTRY plays a crucial role in driving economic growth and connectivity across various sectors. It serves as a catalyst for trade, tourism, and global supply chains, facilitating the movement of goods, services, and people across borders. Within the aviation industry, several sectors have emerged, each contributing to the economic landscape in unique ways.

Healthcare & Pharmaceuticals: The transportation of healthcare products, including pharmaceuticals, is a critical sector within the aviation industry. The timely and efficient delivery of life-saving drugs, vaccines, and medical supplies is essential for public health. However, this sector faces challenges such as maintaining temperature control and complying with strict regulations to ensure the integrity and safety of pharmaceutical products.

Air Ambulance Services: Air ambulance services provide emergency medical transportation for critically ill or injured individuals. These services play a vital role in saving lives by rapidly transporting patients to medical facilities with specialized care. Air ambulances are equipped with medical equipment and staffed by trained healthcare professionals, ensuring the safety and well-being of patients during transit.

Agriculture and Food Transport: The aviation industry also plays a significant role in the transportation of agricultural and food products. Perishable goods, such as fresh produce and seafood, rely on air transportation to maintain their freshness and quality during long-distance journeys. However, the transportation of food products requires adherence to strict safety measures to prevent contamination and ensure food safety.

Manufacturing: Aviation serves as a crucial mode of transportation for manufacturing goods. From automotive components to electronic devices, the aviation industry facilitates the movement of manufactured products across the globe. Just-in-time manufacturing and supply chain management heavily rely on efficient and reliable air transportation to meet tight production schedules.

Technology and Innovation: The aviation industry has embraced technological advancements, leading to the emergence of innovative solutions and services. From digital transformation to the development of multi-functional airline apps, technology plays a vital role in improving operational efficiency, enhancing passenger experiences, and ensuring safety and security in aviation.

Logistics and Supply Chain Management: Efficient logistics and supply chain management are essential for the smooth functioning of the aviation industry. The movement of goods and services requires meticulous planning, coordination, and optimization of resources. From warehousing and distribution to customs clearance and last-mile delivery, effective logistics operations are critical to maintaining a robust and reliable aviation network.

Safety and Security: Safety and security are paramount in the aviation industry. From stringent safety regulations to advanced security measures, ensuring the well-being and protection of passengers, crew, and cargo is of utmost importance. Technology, data analytics, and collaboration among industry stakeholders play a crucial role in continuously enhancing safety and security standards.

In conclusion, the aviation industry encompasses various sectors that contribute to its economic landscape. From healthcare and pharmaceuticals to air ambulance services, agriculture and food transport, manufacturing, technology and innovation, logistics, and safety and security, each sector plays a vital role in shaping the industry's growth and evolution. Understanding the dynamics and challenges within these sectors is crucial for stakeholders in the aviation industry to adapt, innovate, and ensure sustainable economic development.

Sector One: Healthcare & Pharmaceuticals

The transportation of pharmaceuticals via aviation plays a critical role in ensuring the timely and efficient delivery of life-saving drugs and medical supplies to various parts of the world. However, this sector faces several challenges that need to be addressed to maintain the integrity and safety of pharmaceutical products during transit.

One of the primary challenges is maintaining the appropriate temperature conditions throughout the transportation process. Many pharmaceutical products, such as vaccines, biologics, and certain medications, are highly sensitive to temperature variations. Exposure to extreme temperatures can compromise their efficacy and safety, rendering them ineffective or even harmful to patients. This necessitates the implementation of robust temperature control measures during transportation.

Another challenge is the complex regulatory environment surrounding the transportation of pharmaceuticals. Different countries and regions have their own regulations and requirements regarding the handling, storage, and transportation of pharmaceutical products. Compliance with these regulations is essential to ensure product quality, patient safety, and adherence to good distribution practices.

Furthermore, the transportation of pharmaceuticals often involves multiple stakeholders, including manufacturers, freight forwarders, airlines, ground handlers, and customs authorities. Coordinating the activities and ensuring seamless collaboration among these stakeholders is crucial to maintain the integrity of the pharmaceutical supply chain.

Sector Two: Air Ambulance Services

Air ambulance services play a critical role in providing rapid and specialized medical transportation for sick, injured, or medically critical patients. These services involve the use of aircraft, such as airplanes or helicopters, equipped with advanced medical equipment and staffed by certified healthcare professionals, intensive care nurses, and paramedical workers.

The primary objective of air ambulance services is to ensure the safe and efficient transfer of patients from one location to another, often over long distances or in remote areas where ground transportation may not be feasible or timely. The speed and agility of air transportation allow for quick response times, enabling patients to receive the necessary medical care and reach specialized medical facilities in a timely manner.

One of the key benefits of air ambulance services is the ability to provide critical care during the transport process. These aircraft are equipped with advanced medical equipment, such as ventilators, cardiac monitors, defibrillators, and medication supplies, to stabilize and monitor patients throughout the flight. This ensures that patients receive the necessary medical interventions and support during the transportation phase, increasing their chances of a positive outcome.

Another advantage of air ambulance services is the ability to overcome geographical barriers. Air ambulances can reach remote or hard-to-access areas, including rural regions, mountainous terrains, or islands, where ground transportation may be limited or time-consuming. This is particularly beneficial in emergency situations when immediate medical attention is required.

In conclusion, air ambulance services are a crucial component of the healthcare system, providing rapid and specialized medical transportation for patients in need. The ability to access remote areas, provide critical care during transport, and facilitate timely interfacility transfers makes air ambulances invaluable in emergency medical situations. Understanding the different scenarios in which air ambulance services are needed and the advantages of various types of air ambulances ensures efficient and effective patient care and transportation.

Sector Three: Agriculture and Food Transport

Aviation plays a significant role in the transportation of agricultural and food products, enabling the global trade of perishable goods and facilitating the movement of produce from farms to markets around the world. The speed and efficiency of air transportation allow for the timely delivery of fresh and high-value agricultural products, ensuring their quality and reducing the risk of spoilage.

The food trade heavily relies on air cargo services to transport time-sensitive products such as fruits, vegetables, seafood, flowers, and other perishable items. These goods require fast and reliable transportation to maintain their freshness and nutritional value. Airfreight provides a rapid delivery option, especially for long-distance or intercontinental shipments, ensuring that perishable products reach their destinations quickly.

Air transportation also allows for the export and import of food products, supporting international trade in agricultural commodities. It opens up new markets for farmers and enables consumers to access a diverse range of fresh produce from different regions of the world. Additionally, air cargo services provide opportunities for small-scale farmers and businesses to participate in the global food trade by overcoming geographical barriers and connecting them to global markets.

In conclusion, aviation plays a crucial role in the transportation of agricultural and food products, enabling global trade and providing access to fresh produce from different regions. However, there are implications to consider in long-distance food transportation, including cost, environmental impact, and packaging requirements. The transportation of hazardous materials requires adherence to strict safety measures and regulations to protect human health and the environment. By addressing these challenges and implementing sustainable practices, the aviation industry can continue to support the agriculture and food trade while ensuring safety and minimizing its environmental footprint.

Sector Four: Manufacturing

The aviation industry plays a crucial role in the transportation of manufacturing goods. Manufacturers rely on efficient and timely transportation to move their products to various markets around the world. Aviation provides a fast and reliable mode of transportation for high-value and time-sensitive goods, allowing manufacturers to reach global customers quickly and maintain supply chain efficiency.

Air cargo services offered by airlines and dedicated cargo carriers enable manufacturers to transport their goods by air. These services ensure the safe and efficient movement of manufacturing products, including components, parts, finished goods, and specialized equipment. From automotive components to electronic devices, aerospace components to fashion products, aviation facilitates the transportation of a wide range of manufacturing goods.

In conclusion, the aviation industry plays a crucial role in the transportation of manufacturing goods, including the safe handling and transport of dangerous goods. By leveraging the speed, efficiency, global reach, and safety measures of air transportation, manufacturers can effectively meet customer demands, expand their markets, and maintain supply chain resilience.

Emergence of Entrepreneurship in Aviation

With the advancement of technology, there has been a significant rise in the development and popularity of multi-functional airline apps. These apps offer a wide range of services and features to enhance the travel experience for passengers and open up new entrepreneurial opportunities in the aviation industry.

Multi-functional airline apps serve as a one-stop platform where passengers can access various services and information related to their travel. These apps typically include features such as flight booking, check-in, seat selection, real-time flight updates, baggage tracking, loyalty program management, in-flight entertainment, and customer support.

Entrepreneurs in the aviation sector have recognized the potential of these apps and have capitalized on the opportunity to develop and market their own innovative solutions. They create apps that cater to specific niches or provide unique functionalities to differentiate themselves in the market. For example, some apps focus on personalized travel recommendations, airport navigation, language translation, or seamless integration with other travel-related services such as accommodation and car rental.

These entrepreneurial ventures in the airline app space not only provide convenience and value to travelers but also generate revenue through various channels. They may partner with airlines, hotels, travel agencies, and other service providers to offer integrated services and earn commissions or fees. Additionally, they may explore advertising and sponsorship opportunities within their apps to generate additional income.

Expansion of Airline Services through E-Retailing

E-retailing, or online retailing, has experienced rapid growth in recent years, and the aviation industry has embraced this trend to expand its service offerings. Entrepreneurs in aviation have seized the opportunity to leverage e-retailing platforms to provide additional products and services to customers beyond traditional flight tickets.

Airlines now offer e-retailing platforms where passengers can purchase a wide range of products and services related to their travel experience. These platforms enable passengers to conveniently shop for duty-free items, travel essentials, in-flight amenities, travel insurance, airport transfers, and even destination experiences.

Entrepreneurs in the aviation industry have taken advantage of this e-retailing trend to create innovative businesses that cater to specific travel needs or preferences. They may focus on curating unique travel products, such as locally sourced souvenirs or artisanal goods, and offer them through airline e-retailing platforms. Some entrepreneurs may develop specialized services, such as personalized travel concierge services or exclusive access to premium airport lounges, and market them directly to travelers through digital channels.

The expansion of airline services through e-retailing not only provides additional revenue streams for airlines but also offers opportunities for entrepreneurs to create and promote their own brands and products. It enhances the overall travel experience for passengers by providing a seamless and convenient way to access a wide range of travel-related products and services.

In conclusion, the emergence of entrepreneurship in aviation is fueled by the rise of multi-functional airline apps and the expansion of airline services through e-retailing. Entrepreneurs in the industry leverage technology and digital platforms to create innovative solutions, enhance the travel experience, and generate new business opportunities. This entrepreneurial spirit contributes to the continuous growth and evolution of the aviation sector, benefiting both passengers and the industry as a whole.

Conclusion

The aviation industry is influenced by various sectors that play a crucial role in shaping its economic landscape. These sectors include tourism and travel, supply chain management, healthcare and pharmaceuticals, manufacturing, and entrepreneurship.

The tourism and travel sector significantly contributes to the aviation industry's growth and revenue. As people increasingly seek convenient and efficient means of transportation, airlines strive to enhance their services and connectivity to cater to the demands of travelers worldwide.

Supply chain management is another critical sector in aviation. Efficient management of the supply chain is vital for airlines to minimize operating costs, maintain stock accuracy, and provide high-quality services. It involves processes such as equipment acquisition and disposal, sourcing equipment, and ensuring effective maintenance of aircraft and avionics.

Healthcare and pharmaceutical transportation by air require specialized handling and adherence to strict regulations. The transportation of temperature-sensitive pharmaceuticals demands a meticulous operational approach and collaboration across the cold chain partners to maintain the integrity of these critical goods.

Manufacturing goods transportation via air plays a significant role in ensuring the timely delivery of products across the globe. The aviation industry provides a fast and efficient mode of transport for manufacturing goods, allowing businesses to meet customer demands and maintain supply chain efficiency.

The emergence of entrepreneurship in aviation, driven by technology and digital advancements, has opened up new opportunities for innovation and enhanced passenger experiences. Multi-functional airline apps and e-retailing platforms have transformed the way airlines interact with passengers, offering convenience and personalized services.

Logistics, safety, and digital transformation are crucial factors that contribute to the growth and evolution of the aviation industry.

Effective logistics management ensures the smooth operation of airlines and the timely delivery of goods and services. Efficient logistics processes, including inventory management, warehousing, and distribution, play a vital role in reducing costs, optimizing resources, and meeting customer demands.

Safety is of utmost importance in the aviation industry. Airlines and regulatory authorities prioritize stringent safety measures to protect passengers, crew, and cargo. Compliance with safety regulations, robust maintenance practices, and continuous training of personnel contribute to maintaining a high level of safety standards in aviation.

Digital transformation is revolutionizing the aviation industry, offering opportunities for improved efficiency, enhanced customer experiences, and cost optimization. The adoption of digital technologies, such as airline apps, e-retailing platforms, data analytics, and automation, allows airlines to streamline operations, personalize services, and make data-driven decisions.

The integration of digital solutions in areas like aircraft maintenance, flight operations, and passenger services enhances operational efficiency, reduces manual processes, and enables proactive maintenance practices. It also enables airlines to leverage data for predictive analytics, optimizing flight routes, fuel consumption, and passenger demand.

In conclusion, the aviation industry's growth and evolution are influenced by sectors such as tourism, supply chain management, healthcare, manufacturing, and entrepreneurship. Logistics, safety, and digital transformation are key enablers of this growth, ensuring efficient operations, passenger safety, and enhanced experiences. As the aviation industry continues to evolve, these factors will remain essential for its success in an increasingly connected and technology-driven world.

LESSON 8:

Sectors Shaping Aviation's Economic Future

Introduction: Aviation as the Economy's Silent Engine

Aviation is more than planes and airports it is the backbone of global trade, healthcare logistics, agriculture exports, manufacturing supply chains, and digital innovation. Each flight supports multiple industries, creating ripple effects that transform local economies. For Africa, aviation is not only a transport system but also a development engine, enabling access to markets, medicine, and opportunity.

Deep Dive: Sectors Powered by Aviation

1. **Healthcare & Pharmaceuticals:** Timely delivery of vaccines, medicines, and equipment relies on secure, temperature-controlled aviation logistics.
2. **Air Ambulance Services:** Life-saving emergency flights bridge the gap

between patients and specialized medical facilities.

3. **Agriculture & Food Transport:** Fresh produce, seafood, and flowers reach global markets via air cargo, sustaining farmers and exporters.

4. **Manufacturing & Supply Chains:** Just-in-time production depends on reliable cargo and component transport.

5. **Technology & Entrepreneurship:** Multi-functional airline apps, e-retailing, and digital platforms create new aviation-linked businesses.

6. **Logistics & Security:** Warehousing, customs clearance, and robust security protocols are critical to the aviation economy.

Case Study: *Kenya's horticulture industry* relies on aviation to deliver roses and fresh produce to Europe within 24 hours. Without efficient air cargo, thousands of jobs and billions in exports would vanish.

Exercises

1. **Sector Mapping:** Pick one sector (healthcare, food, manufacturing). Write a one-page essay on how aviation supports it in your country.
2. **Business Idea:** Brainstorm one aviation-linked business (e.g., drone spraying for farms, air cargo logistics, app-based passenger services). Outline how it could make money.
3. **Impact Chain:** Draw a diagram showing how a single passenger flight supports jobs in catering, hotels, retail, tourism, and logistics.

Action Framework: Tapping Into Aviation-Linked Sectors

1. **Identify Growth Hubs:** Research which industries in your country (tourism, agriculture, mining, tech) rely most on aviation.
2. **Build Cross-Sector Skills:** If in healthcare, learn supply chain logistics;

if in agriculture, study cold-chain systems.

3. **Think Export-Ready:** Identify products that can reach global markets faster with aviation (seafood, flowers, crafts).
4. **Leverage Digital:** Explore e-retailing, apps, and online platforms to create new aviation-related ventures.
5. **Collaborate:** Seek partnerships across aviation, tourism, logistics, and manufacturing sectors to unlock joint opportunities.

Reflection Journal

- Which aviation-linked sector excites me the most, and why?
- What local product or service in my country could benefit from aviation access?
- If I launched a business tomorrow, how could I design it around aviation-linked opportunities?

CONCLUSION:

READY FOR TAKEOFF – YOUR FUTURE AWAITS

As we bring this journey through the skies of aviation to the short finals as we touch down, it is important to pause and reflect on what lies before us. Aviation is not merely about aircraft or airports; it is a living ecosystem that powers economies, creates jobs, saves lives, and connects dreams across borders. It is the invisible thread weaving together healthcare, agriculture, manufacturing, tourism, technology, and security binding our world into one global community.

Throughout these chapters, we have explored the vast dimensions of aviation:

- From the **beginner's guide** that demystified careers beyond piloting.
- To the **global and African context** that revealed the continent's untapped potential.
- To the power of **management, leadership, and human resources** in shaping resilient organizations.
- To the role of **marketing, technology, and entrepreneurship** in driving competitiveness.
- And finally, to the many **sectors that aviation fuels**, making it the backbone of modern economies.

The lesson is clear: aviation is not a closed industry reserved for a privileged few. It is a dynamic space where students, entrepreneurs, innovators, policy makers, and dreamers can all find their place.

Africa's Skies: From Potential to Reality

Africa, with its youthful population, abundant resources, and strategic location, holds the greatest aviation opportunity of the

21st century. Forecasts predict over **350 million passengers annually by 2038,** but the true story lies beyond numbers. Every passenger represents a job supported, a business enabled, a family connected, or a life saved. Every cargo flight carries not just goods, but opportunities for farmers, manufacturers, and traders. Every drone delivery carries with it the promise of a healthier, more connected future.

But potential alone is not enough. Africa's aviation story will only be written if young people, governments, and entrepreneurs step forward with courage. This requires investment in training, infrastructure, innovation, and above all leadership.

The Role of Technology and Innovation

The digital revolution is already transforming aviation. Biometrics, blockchain, drones, green fuels, and artificial intelligence are no longer distant possibilities they are realities shaping our airports and airlines. For Africa, the ability to **leapfrog outdated**

systems and embrace new technologies offers a unique advantage. Those who learn, adapt, and innovate will lead.

The Human Element: People Remain the Engines of Aviation

Aircraft may define the industry, but people sustain it. Engineers, dispatchers, flight attendants, auditors, safety officers, managers, and entrepreneurs form the backbone of aviation. Without skilled, passionate, and ethical professionals, no aircraft would take off. That is why human resource development through mentorship, training, and leadership is the single most important investment any nation or company can make.

Your Role in This Journey

This book is not meant to be the end of your exploration; it is the beginning. The chapters were designed as a runway preparing you for takeoff. What happens next depends on you. Ask yourself:

- What excites me most in aviation?

- What skills or knowledge must I build?
- How can I position myself in this fast-changing industry?

Whether you are a student seeking a career, an entrepreneur searching for opportunity, or a professional considering leadership, remember: **the aviation industry needs you.**

A Call to Action

- **To young people:** Dream boldly. The aviation world is bigger than you think. Step in with curiosity and courage.
- **To entrepreneurs:** See beyond planes see logistics, apps, cargo, e-retailing, drones. Build solutions that matter.
- **To governments:** Prioritize aviation as infrastructure for growth. Support training, policy reforms, and investment.
- **To professionals:** Lead with integrity. Mentor the next generation. Build organizations that outlive you.

Final Reflection

The title of this book, *Ready for Takeoff*, is more than a metaphor it is a declaration. The runway is clear. The engines are powered. Africa's aviation industry, and indeed the global industry, is poised for unprecedented growth.

But the question is: **Are you ready?**

The future of aviation will not be shaped by those who watch from the sidelines, but by those who dare to board, navigate turbulence, and chart new routes. My hope is that this book has equipped you with the knowledge, inspiration, and tools to not only join this industry but to transform it.

Your sky is not the limit it is your creation space. The world is waiting. The seatbelt signs are off. The horizon is wide open.

It's time for you to take off.

ABOUT THE AUTHOR

GRACE KIMANI IS A STALWART leader and aviation industry veteran, boasting over two decades of hands-on experience and expertise. Her roots trace back to a quaint village named Kinangop, nestled within the Nyandarua County of Kenya. This unassuming beginning forged her resilience and strength, becoming the bedrock of her stellar career.

As an acclaimed customer experience practitioner and an esteemed expert in aviation facilitation, Grace's contributions to the industry have garnered several awards. She has established herself as a guiding force in the aviation industry, particularly through her visionary initiative, N-GOAL. This platform seeks to bridge the gap between students, parents, air operators, and entrepreneurs by connecting them to the aviation market. Through a combination of mentorship, sensitization, and publications, N-GOAL aims to raise awareness about the vast array of careers and business opportunities available within the aviation industry.

Grace holds a master's degree in Project Management, a testament to her academic prowess. Over the years, she has pursued and completed a range of leadership courses from various institutions, honing her leadership abilities. As a certified trainer in facilitation (Annex 9), and as an auditor in aviation, she possesses a formidable suite of skills. Furthermore, she's a recognized Social Change Advocate committed to advancing the

Sustainable Development Goals and promoting economic growth through education and innovation development.

Grace maintains active memberships in the Customer Experience Professional body, ICX Kenya, and the globally recognized Women in Aviation International. These affiliations serve as platforms for her to network, share her knowledge, and raise awareness about the myriad opportunities available in the aviation industry.

Visionary and ambitious, Grace aspires to inspire and make a profound impact on one million students and entrepreneurs across Africa by 2030 . Her goal is to help them package themselves competitively and position themselves globally as the next generation of aviation leaders. Her mission is clear to shape the future leaders of the aviation industry, and by extension, propel the growth and success of the industry itself.

www.ingramcontent.com/pod-product-compliance
Lightning Source LLC
Chambersburg PA
CBHW021800190326
41518CB00007B/384